CARE H[illegible] STAFF TRAINING

Food hygi[illegible] ealth

and Saf[illegible] nd bereavement

ACTIVITIES

INFECTION

DEMENTIA

FIRE

FIRST AID

FOOD HYGIENE

MANUAL

HANDLING

MEDICATION

MENTAL

ILLNESS

HEALTH

& SAFETY

Compiled by

James Safo

BA (Hons) law, account Psychiatric

and General nurse, Cert ed. V1,A1,Certificate

in First aid, Food hygiene, manual handling Dip Health

management Health and Safety, Fire safety

QUICK SEARCH

Quick search		2
Copy Right/Reserve		3
Dedication/acknowledgement		4
Preface		5
Author/Qualification		6-9

Chapt. Topic	Content Page	Knowledge Page
1 Dying, death Bereavement	10-12	49-73
2 Medication	13-19	74- 180
3 Infection	20-23	181-204
4 Food Hygiene	24-27	205-240
5 First Aid	28-31	241-267
6 Manual Handling	32-33	268-277
7 Health & Safety (Over 185 Q & A)	34-48	278-384
Reference		385
Index		388

Disclaimer (Exclusive clause)

The author and all employees disclaim any incorrect interpretation wrong answers to questions or text, harm include emotional, psychological, and physical or any form of harm to the reader/listener or being given information by third parties.

Furthermore, this disclaimer protects all contributory people, directors, employees, 3rd party, and author and will not be liable for any injury caused.

Dedication

I dedicate this book to all my children who suffered with me and still we remain strong and united.

Acknowledgements

The real author of all my books is Almighty God/Allah/Parama Nandha who through his messengers. I was not capable of neither writing books or achieving those high-powered qualifications: physically, 75% of my bones are in the advanced stage of arthritis, I have the worst type of cardiovascular disease, a large heart (hypertrophy), chronic depression and anxiety and, worst of all, three out of four of my brain lobes have been damaged since 1998 as a result of a serious car accident. Yet I rose to be one of the most successful international entrepreneurs in the world, miscarriage stripped my millions, and now come back to be more than what I had. This is an evidence of God's power against enemies. I believe my rising to the top, miscarriage strip me of everything, recovered to have much more what than I had, make me living memory of Prophets Job and Joseph replica in the Bible and the Quran.

Preface

As a qualified psychiatric and General trained nurse, BA (Hons) law and account) etc, and having own about ten (include 6 care homes at one stage) business at the same time in United Kingdom for over twenty-five years. I hope this book together with my other book How to set up care home and care agencies, management of care homes and care agencies and other books as listed in this book; will give more insight to all carers to be aware of knowledge and in the care environment irrespective of the sector or category of care being given.

You need to have formal training to obtain certificate of competence from approved training organisation, this publication is to make you aware of recommendation and requirement for carer, irrespective of care sector. All care homes and agencies need to have specific training manual on the premises so that the staff can refer to them at any time.

Due diligence

About the Author

I was an abandon child at the age of four. As an adult I became a high-profile international entrepreneur based in England for over twenty-five years and owned ten different businesses at the same time, including an international college, and at one stage owned about 6 care homes at the same time. I wrote all document needed to set up and manage them successful. etc. I was arguably one of the most successful black people in Europe at the time,

My areas of Qualification

LLM(Master of Law o/g)

Legal researcher (master level)

Business, CSR and business human Right (master level)

1. BA (Hons) , Law: include Criminal, Tort, damages, Contract, Property, Equity and Trust, European law, Public, Constitutional, Judicial Review
2. On Master of Law level; which is on -going, but I have passed the module " legal research", and "business, CSR Corporate social responsibility and human Right law"
3. Advance Dip. Business Law, Level 4: include Employment, Agency, Damages, Tort, Contract, employment tribunal etc.
4. Dip. Criminology
5. BA (Hons)op. Account: Financial Accountant and Management Accountant
6. Cert. Acct; Professional Certificate in Financial and Management Accounting
7. Dip. Book-keeping, Level 3
8. Nursing: RMN Psychiatry trained nurse
9. General Trained Nurse
10. Cert. in Education (Lecturer)
11. Business Certificate in Advanced Management

12. Cert. Business Enterprise
13. Advanced Food Hygiene
14. Intermediate Health and Safety
15. Dip. Safety Management
16. International Entrepreneur for over 25 years
17. Computers: Cert. Cisco Level 2 Technician, (build, repair, networking)
18. Dip. Clait Plus (in all software)
19. New Clait Dip. Level 2
20. Microsoft Specialist
21. ECDL Level 2
22. Script writing: Dip. TV, radio, stage and film
23. Non-fiction writing: Dip. Autobiography, Biography and Family History
24. Cert. in Counselling
25. Author/Self-Publisher: Over 12 books (with some yet to be published)
26. Plumbing: Level 3 City and Guild
27. Theology: Cert. Bible studies; researched Theology for my PhD (most faiths)
28. Psychology and Social Science (Level 1 at university)

29. Photographer: Portrait, Glamour and Figure Photographer (PGFP).

30. Dip. Hypnotherapy

31. National Vocation Qualification (NVQ); Internal Verifier, Trainer and Assessor

32. 2018-2020: University Student of LLM (Master of Laws)

33. Author Publisher of over 25titles books by January 2020

CONTENT

Chapter 1 Approx. page47-71

DEATH, DYING AND BEREAVEMENT

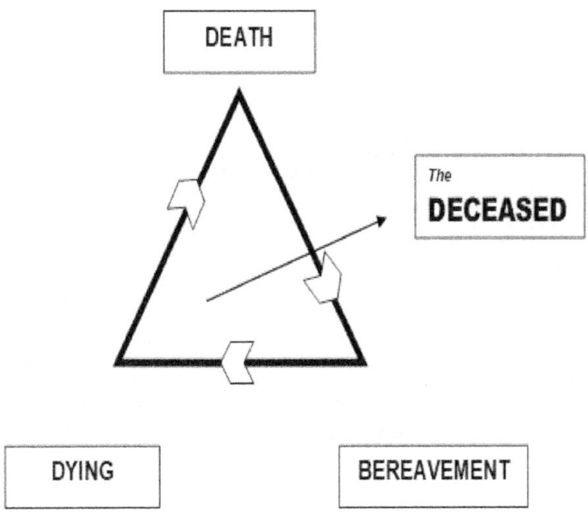

Dying, Death Bereavement

Introduction

- Loss
- Culture and Religion
- Medicalisation
- Do Not Resuscitate
- Euthanasia

Dying

- Responding to Dying
- The Dying Person's Perspective
- Communication and Dying
- Making Decisions
- Death Approaches ….
- Fear
- "How Will I Die?
- Symptoms of Dying
- Pain and Dying
- Weakness
- Breathlessness
- Loss of Appetite

- Nausea and Vomiting
- Constipation
- Water Retention
- Confusion
- The End is Nigh

Death

- Immediately After Death
- Sudden Unexpected Death
- Removing the Body
- Registering Death
- Funeral Arrangements
- Who Needs Informing?
- Organ Donation

Bereavement

- After the Death
- Reacting to Grief
- Mourning
- Grieving

Chapter; 2; Medication   72-197

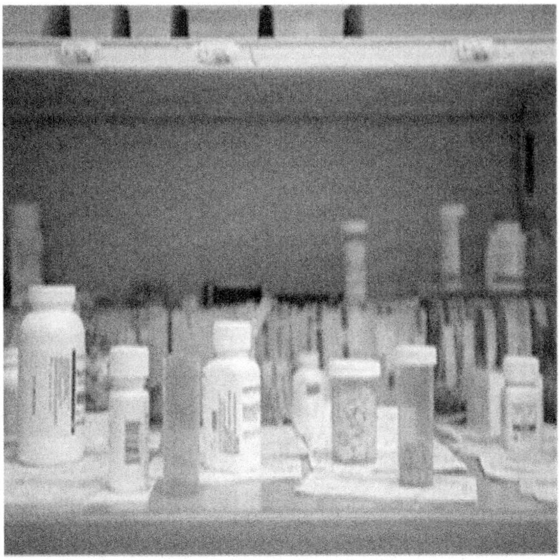

Benefiting from Training,
Purpose
Introduction,
Terminology
Sources of Information,
Whilst Being Trained
Length of Training,
Legislation
Employee's Responsibilities
Hazardous Substances
What is Medication?
Drugs
Why Do We Use Medication
How Do Drugs Work,
How Drugs Affect Us
Adverse Reactions:
Interactions
Oral Medication,
Inhaled Medication
The three main types of injection are:
Types of Medication,
Medication Policy
Section 2 – Drug Groups,
Analgesics (painkillers)
Antacids,
Anti-angina:

Anti-anxiety (tranquillisers):

Anti-arrhythmic,

Anti-cancer:

Anti-convulsions:

Ant-depressants:

Anti-diarrhoeal:

Anti-emetics

Anti-hypertensive,

Ant-psychotics

Anti-rheumatics,

Anti-ulcer

Antibiotics,

Antihistamines

Antiseptics,

Beta-blockers

Bronchodilators

Corticosteroids (steroids):

Diabetes Drugs:

Diuretics:

Immunosuppressant:

Inflammatory Bowel Disease (IBD)

Laxatives,

Lipid Lowering:

Menstrual Disorders:

Migraine,

Muscle Relaxants:

Sleeping Medication (hypnotics):

Stimulants:

Vasodilators:

Vitamins,

Non-prescription Medication

Drugs and Clients,

Infants and Children

Pregnant Women:

Elderly Persons:

Know Your Medications,

Medical Register

Giving Advice,

Contraindications

Adverse Effects,

Allergies

Drug Tolerance,

Dependence

Physical Dependence:,

Medication Reviews

The review should include:

Clients New to Our Service

Client Leaving Our Care,

Before Drug Administration

Record Keeping,

Recording Refused Medication

Pharmacy Records,

Prescriptions

Authorisation to Change Medication

Labels,

Presentation

Supplying Medication,

Who Owns the Medication?

Medication Receipt

Medication –

Stock Management

Stock Checks,

Storage

Underestimating the Size,

Security:

Homecare- Medicine Cabinets

Drug Administration,

Infection Control

Medication Trolley (Cart),

security is essential

Interruptions and Distractions

Labelling,

Manual Administration Records
Important Terminology,
Medication Administration
Refusal,
Doctors and MAR Sheets
Eating and Drinking,
Liquid Medication
Crushing Medication,
Convert Medication
Emergency situations:,
Missing a Dose
Exceeding a Dose,
Disposal and Consent
non-oral administration,
Specialised Techniques
Signs, Regulators
Emergencies:,
Storage
Leaks,
Eye Medication (Drops)
Ear Medication, Nasal drops
Inserting an Inhaler,
Vital Signs
Breathing Assessment,
Measuring Blood Pressure
Taking a Pulse,
Controlled Drugs

Authorisation to Administer,

Handling Illegal Drugs

Controlled Drugs (CD) Disposal

Self-Medication,

error management

Some important principles

What is a medication error?

Chapter 3 198-223

INFECTION CONTROL

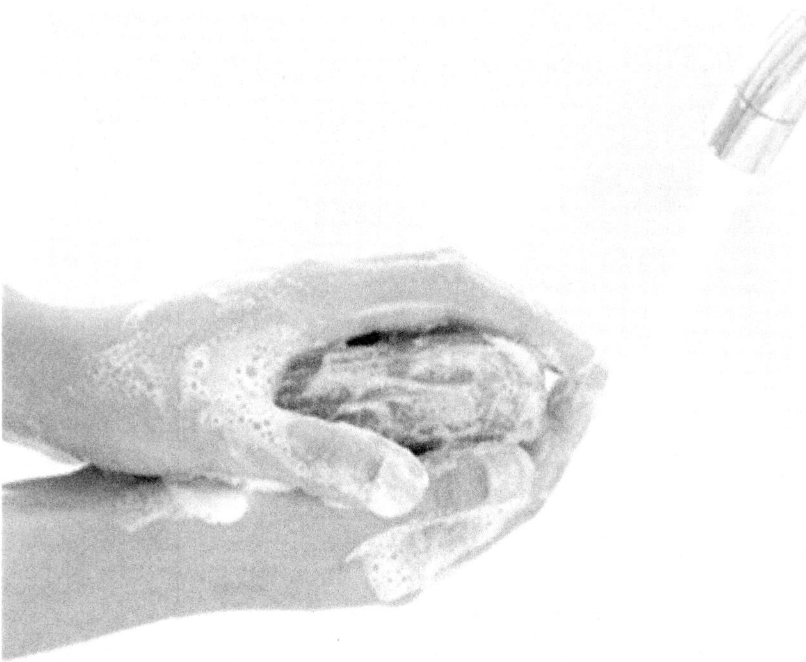

Content

Legislation

At Risk Groups

Legislation

Employer's Responsibilities

The Law in Practice

Reporting of Injuries and Diseases

Substances Hazardous to Health

Micro-organisms

Viruses

Bacteria

Chain of Infection

Means of Transmission

Risk Assessment

Hand Washing

Types of Hand Decontamination

Handwashing Technique

Dry Your Hands Properly

Skin Care

Physical Decontamination

Environmental Cleanliness

Cleaning Schedule

Cleaning

Drying

Disinfecting Using Chemicals

Sterilisation

Cleaning Up A Spillage

Sharps

Needlestick Policy

Specimens

Personal Protective Equipment

Barrier Precautions

Isolation

Personal Hygiene

Staff and Visitor Toilet Facilities

Uniforms

Linen and Laundry

Lighting and ventilation

Sluicing

Clinical Waste

General Waste

Pets and Pests

Communicable Diseases

Chapter 4 224-259

FOOD HYGIENE

Content

Food Hygiene

The Law- What it Requires

The Law- Legal Duties

The Law- Enforcement

Food Hygiene Policy

The Significance of Food Hygiene

Food Poisoning- At Risk Groups

Food Hazards

Bacteria

Binary Fission

Food

The Danger Zone

Temperature Guidelines

Food Delivery

Food Storage

Food Preparation

Food Cooking

Food Cooling

Food Holding…

Food Re-heating

Food Serving

Personal Hygiene

Skin

Hair

Mouth, nose, ears

Using the toilet

Toiletries etc

Jewellery

Clothing

Cuts and Grazes

Diarrhoea and Vomiting

Hand Washing

Pets and Pests

Premises

Equipment

Food equipment

Work surfaces

Cleaning & Disinfection

Chemicals

Dishwashers.

Waste disposal

Outdoor bins

Cleaning schedule

Summary of Food Safety

Chapter 5 260-288

FIRST AID

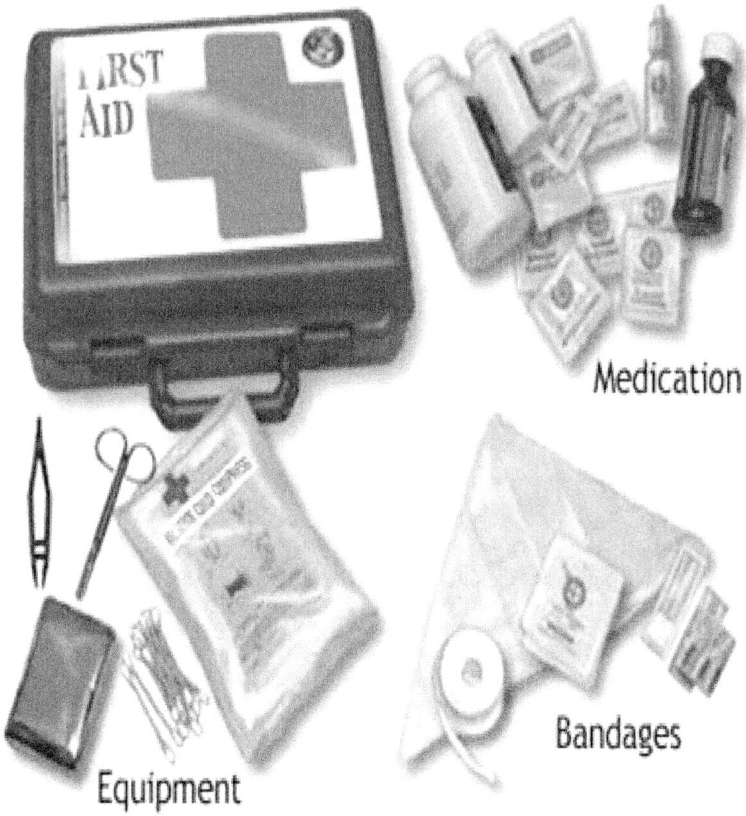

First Aid Training

Don’t Make Matters Worse

Don’t Make Matters Worse

Whilst Waiting For Help

Reassure Them

Moving a Casualty

Airway

Breathing

Circulation

Recovery Position

Accident Procedure

Accident Books

Reporting of Injuries and Diseases

After The Accident

First Aid Boxes

Universal Infection Control Procedures

Bleeding

Nose Bleeding

Cuts and Grazes

Fractured Bone

Hip Fracture

Strains and Sprains

Ice Packs

Dressings

Bandages

Chemical Burns

Sunburn

Swallowed Substances

Drug Poisoning

Electrocution

Heart Attack

Stroke

Seizures / Fits

Shock

Anaphylactic Shock

Asthma Attack

A chocking Adult

Vomiting and Diarrhoea

Earache

Diabetes

Hypothermia

Bites and Stings

Traffic Incidents

Chapter 6 289-298

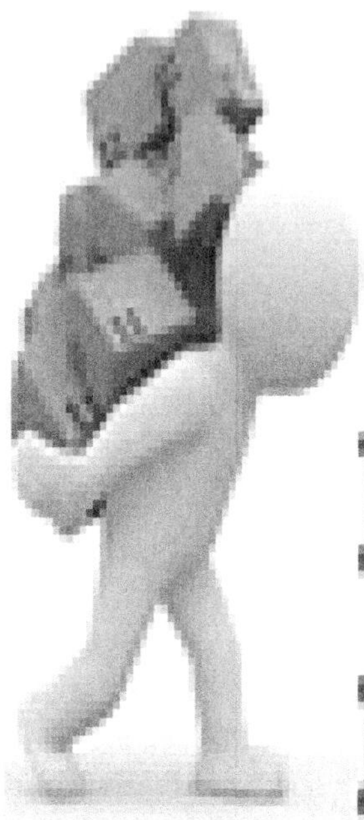

Manual Handling

Safety management/Manual Handling

Employers Duties Will:

Employees also have duties to;

Assessing the risk

favourable conditions.

Good handling

Stop and think

Position the feet

Get a firm grip

Keep close to the load

Don't jerk

position the feet

Put down, adjust

injury?

Chapter 7 Pages 299-399

HEALTH AND SAFETY

187 Questions and Answers.

Please attempt to answer some of these questions before you check the answers

Content

1) **Q;** Describe the role of the supervisor in accident prevention 1
2) **Q;** Write notes on factors that could Couse employee to commit unsafe acts in the work place. 2
3) **Q;** How does stress affect employee? 2
4) **Q;** How many parties involved in accidents prevention at work? 3
5) **Q**; Name some third party and equipment that could contribute to accident at work? 3
6) **Q;** what is good house keeping
7) **Q;** Who is responsible for good housekeeping?
8) **Q**: What is the aim and objective of good housekeeping? 4

9) **Q;** Explain Good house keeping

10) **Q**: what is the benefit of good housekeeping?.

11) **Q**: What is the benefit of doing things in orderliness manner

12) **Q**; What difference altitude of employee who work in clean environment and one in dirty?

13) **Q;** What are important issue to have in the environment?

14) **Q;** Why are special precaution needed for health and Safety?

15) **Q;** How are liquid and chemical stored?

16) **Q:** When are faulty circuits a factor?

17) **Q:** Name some issues that employee be trained?

18) **Q:** Name some issues that employee be trained?

19) **Q:** Explain what preventive measures should be taken?

20) **Q;** How should chemical be used?

21) **Q:** what precaution on electric and tools use?

22) **Q;** which area that no smoking sign is a must?

23) **Q;** What is risk assessment?

24) **Q**: What is safe systems of work?

25) **Q;** Where is the motivation important?

26) **Q** :briefly outline the major causes of fires at the work place?

27)Q; List five reasons why in certain instances protective equipment and clothing is not worn?

28)Q; Write short notes on six health hazards detrimental to the health of workers?.

29)Q: What is the aim of using PPE

30)Q: What is the requirements for protective clothing and equipment?

31)Q: Name some (PPE) types of physical protective equipment available

32)Q; What is PPE made from?

33) Q; Why is it important to protect external skin?

34)Q; Give example of law

35)Q; What PPE are used for people working in dangerous environment?

36)Q; Who supply PPE at work?

37)Q: What happen if employee have accident at work?

38)Q; Will PPE give total protection from injury?

39) Q; What would occur if there was a lack of management control?

40)Q; why should an accident prevention programme start with top management?

41)Q; Clearly define organisational policy.?

42) Q; Clearly Delineated Standards for management work.

43)Q; Evaluate individual performance

44)Q; Why is use of self-appraisals important?

45)Q; Explain measurement of control

46)Q; Fully describe the aims of a safety training programme

47)Q what is safety committee's function?

48)Q; Describe your understanding of Disaster?

49)Q; What should safety committee promote?

50)Q; Give an example of disaster

51)Q; Name two important points to remember when coping with an emergency and explain why you have chosen these two points in

52)Q; List five steps you should take upon finding a fire in a building.

53)Q; Why children should be wrapped in a blanket during a fire.

54)Q; What is emergency manual?

A: An emergency manual is the organization/s policy of what to do

55)Q; List the content of an emergency manual and explain why you feel they are an important part of the manual

56)Q; What is Civil Defence Legislation?

57)Q; Name some issues it covers?

58)Q; What are the two civil legislation?

59) Q; What and why was civil contingence secretariat (CCS) form?

60) Q; What is local authorities responsibilities in CCS

61) Q; What prompted enaction of civil protection and Peace act?

62)Q: Summarise the Aberfan disaster?

63)Q; Describe the sea Express oil spill?

64)Q; What was the impact of the environment as result of Sea Express?

65)Q: How was the Sea express disaster dealt with?

66)Q; List five important aspects that an organisation should established to minimise effect of a "disaster? Explain these points

67)67) **Q;** Explain your approach to a bomb threat.

68)Q; what safety report for board of directors

69) Q; What should mission statement of organisation on Safety issues be?

70)Q; How is on the job health measures?

71)Q; What must alcohol and drugs in the report state?

72) Q: Explain loss of control programmed?

73)Q; What must be done on staff induction on (COSHH)?

74) Q; How should organisation deals with First Aid?

75)Q; What include good physical working conditions?

76) What is the important of sanitation?

77) Q; What are some health risks?

78)Q; What is AIDS ?

79)Q: How is Aids transmit?

80)Q; Can Aids is Preventable

81)Q; What must organisation do regarding AID?

82)Q; How should cafeteria be kept?

83)Q; Give an example of how organisation could conclude their report.

84)Q; How do organisations deals with duty of care

85)Q; Write summary of safety management course

86)Q: where is Health and Safety important?

87)Q: what is the 0ne of the most important to consider before start work?

88)Q; summary employers responsibility

89)Q; summary of employee responsibility

90)Q; What is Hazard -

91) Q; summarise how to deal with electricity at work?

92)Q: Explain Classes of Fire

93)Q; When must hose not to be used?

94)Q; What is fire evacuation procedure

95)Q; summarise how to deal with Fire prevention at work?

96)Q; Explain personal protective equipment

97)Q; what happen if employee refused to use PPE.

98)Q: What type of PPE and management responsibility on it.

99)Q; What must organisation do in major emergency

100) **Q:** why is it important to have first aid at work?

101) **Q;** why should organisation have basic rules

102) **Q;** What is the likelihood that harm may occur?

103) **Q;** Explain RIDDOR

104) **Q;** Explain COSHH

105) **Q;** What does COSHH include?

106) **Q;** Give summary of some manual handling

107) **Q;** Give summary of how to lift load safely?

108) **Q;** Who need to be trained first in organisation.

109) **Q;** summarise how you will be able to utilise these theories when working in every day situation.

110) **Q**; How do some employee become more risk due to extra income

111) **Q;** How do some employee become more risk due Security of their job

112) **Q**; How do some employee become more risk due to Seeking approval of others

113) **Q**: How do some employee become more risk due to extra income Difficulties in Inattention

114) Q; What is the effect of Job-related Conditions on employee?

115) **Q;** How can frustration in an employee be noticed?

116) **Q;** What is one way to alleviate employee problems?

117) **Q;** How can employee be affected by Perceptual Difficulties

118) **Q;** What is the role and functions of the manager in the prevention of accidents.

119) **Q;** Functions of the Supervisor in the prevention of accidents.

120) **Q;** Why should the supervisor be held responsible for accident prevention?

121) **Q:** steps be taken in safety training

122) **Q** What must the manager or supervisor do to make sure the employee have absorbed lectures

123) **Q;** what is the meaning of loss pf control

124) **Q:** What is the definition loss control

125) **Q;** How many phases to lose control?

126) **Q;** What is the main aim of loss of control?

127) **Q;** What is the consequence of unsafe act and condition at work place?

128) **Q;** What is the term “Creative” in health and safety?

129) **Q;** How can supervisor find out the cause of accident.

130) **Q;** what is the next step when the cause established?

131) **Q;** Is it possible to fail to establish the Couse of accident through corrective interview?

132) **Q**; what must employer do if the suspected employee is unhelpful?

133) **Q**; Can employee unsafe behaviour be changed?

134) **Q;** Name few causes of incidents

135) **Q;** In business, how is incident downgraded?

136) **Q;** Briefly describe People cause or downgrade accidents.

137) **Q:** Briefly describe equipment as cause or downgrade accidents.

138) **Q:** Briefly describe material people as cause or downgrade accidents.

139) **Q;** Briefly describe environment as cause or downgrade accidents.

140) **Q;** What are remedies of accidents

141) **Q:** Who is responsibility for accident prevention ?

142) **Q:** What are the cost of accidents.

143) **Q;** What is the Cost to the Victim

144) **Q;** What is the Cost to the Company in accident?

145) **Q;** What is the Cost of accident to the Nation

146) **Q**; What is the cost to the company Manager

147) **Q;** How can loss control be enhanced?

148) **Q;** Briefly describe Safety Audit as loss of control remedy

149) **Q:** Briefly describe Safety survey as loss of control remedy

150) **Q**: Briefly describe Safety tour as loss of control remedy.

151) **Q;** Briefly describe Safety sampling as loss of control remedy

152) **Q:** Briefly describe Scheduled Safety Inspection

153) **Q:** Briefly describe controlling losses by teaching people as means of loss of control remedy.

154) **Q;** Briefly describe Readiness as means to loss of control remedy

155) **Q;** Briefly describe Association as means to loss of control remedy

156) **Q:** Briefly describe Application as means to loss of control remedy

157) **Q**; What is the seriousness of losses and the necessity for loss control.

158) **Q;** who is responsible to alert health risk?

159) **Q;** what equipment must organisation health care have to provide total health care for employee

160) **Q:** Name some health risk which can be found at work place?

161) **Q**: Give an example of Colour Coding for Safety Identification in a factory?

162) Q: Why is it important to have proper factory Layout.

163) Q; Name few things to improve factory layout?

164) **Q**; What are the rules in handling of Ladders?

165) **Q:** What precaution must be taken concerning electricity?

166) **Q;** What precaution to be made on Company Vehicles

167) **Q:** Describe some machines that need guard.

168) **Q;** What equipment in machine mechanism might cause hazard?

169) **Q;** What is machine guard?

170) **Q:** Why should machines be safeguarded?

171) **Q**: What materials is used for machine guards?

172) **Q**: Name some types of machine guards.

173) **Q:** What is requirements of machine guards?

174) **Q;** How do machine guards help?

175) **Q;** How does Angle grinder works?

176) **Q;** What precaution for machine guards for electrical equipment?

177) **Q:** What precaution to be taken for portable electrical tools and equipment?

178) **Q;** How do you warn employee of faulty electrical equipment or machine?

179) **Q:** What hazards can electrical apparatus cause?

180) **Q**; What causes faulty electrical circuits?

181) **Q:** What can radiation cause

182) **Q**: What is the advantage of good Ventilation

183) **Q:** What precaution for Power Failures?

184) **Q:** What to do if refuse is not remove

185) **Q:** What you must do in Hurricanes

186) **Q;** What to do in Earthquakes

187) **Q;** What happened in Flood

Chapter 1 Pages 47-71

DEATH, DYING AND BEREAVEMENT

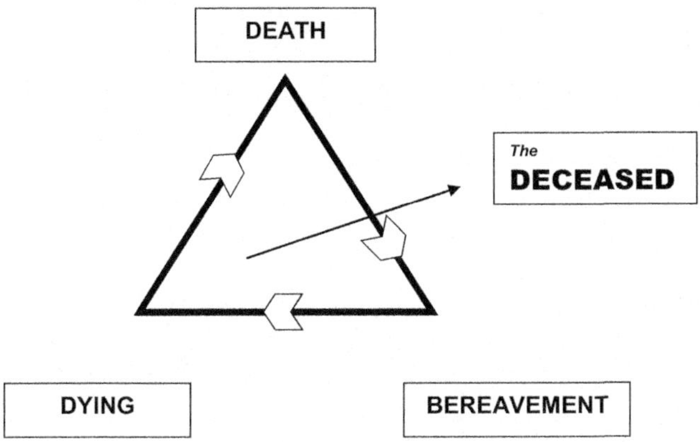

Introduction

Below is summary of the topic

Key; Home is referred to as the environment.

It is highly likely, in many caring environments, you will have to cope with the death of a service user/and/or the bereavement of a person coping with the death of someone close to them.

To do this is a team effort, we need to work together, and caring in such circumstances will require: □ Communication skills □ Professionalism □ Ethical practice

Important Note:

It is possible some of this training resource may be sensitive for you; your feelings may be aroused by some of the issues raised.

If you are affected by any of the material, you must talk to someone about it immediately, preferably your manager or supervisor, who can take steps to support you. It is not shameful to ask for support when dealing with the emotions and feelings of dying, death and bereavement but, since this is triggered in the context of care related training, a sign of good professional judgement.

Loss

The home society is less accustomed to death and loss than at any time in the past discussing dying and death doesn't happen. Often, when the subject of death is mentioned, people: □ feel uncomfortable □ say it is depressing □ don't want to be reminded □ change the subject

Yet, one certainty in life is that we are all going to die and that means those left behind will experience loss, in some way or other.

Generally, most people die in hospital because that is the way we deal with dying nowadays, the family can't cope, and death is often seen as a "medical thing".

Until relatively recently, to have a dead body laid out in the front room would have been quite normal. Today, most people would consider doing that slightly odd. This shows how death, and being able to address loss, has changed.

Since fewer people die at home, we have less to do with death personally, which makes it less familiar.

This does not reduce the sense of loss when the reality of death happens to us; if anything, it makes the sense of loss worse.

Our Christian-based culture is mostly eroded; therefore, our understanding of death has changed, which also makes the sense of loss worse.

30% of people in care homes die every year; they seem to just “disappear” and staff can feel neutral to death – the sense of loss itself can seem lost.

Loss and the Service User

Most elderly service users will have probably experienced death and loss far more closely than those of us in our middle years and younger: □ loss through the death of a loved one, friend, relative, etc. losing their home □ losing some or all of their freedom.

They may have experienced health loss, for example: hearing □ mental capability □ mobility □ sight □ speech.

Culture and Religion

To expect us to understand every detail of everybody’s culture and religion is unrealistic. However, we do need to understand basic elements of the cultures and religions of those we care for and those close to them with regards to how they see death. For example, will they see death as:

joyous? □ lonely? □ relief? □ terrifying?

We need to know because this will not only affect their practical preparations but their emotional responses as well. We need to plan how to prepare in order that we can ensure consistent quality of care to all those we have a duty to in circumstances that may be difficult.

Medicalisation

Our society sees medical involvement with dying and death as the normal and proper way – death is seen as a medical condition rather than a physical reality or spiritual state.

It is probable you will have active involvement with someone who is definitely going to die; caring for them could involve:

them coming to terms with the inevitability of death □ seeking to maintain their self-worth □ struggling with maintaining independence □ finding ways to encourage the person to make choices □

pain control psychological support spiritual support supporting those close to them.

These types of support and caring, albeit these are just some of the issues, are often known as palliative care.

Do Not Resuscitate

Our society sees death as a medical matter where choice, quality of life, the value of medication, etc. can all be “thrown into the pot” when deciding the time and manner of death.

A Service User might express the wish not to be resuscitated if that situation were to arise. You must inform the Registered Manager who will make this known to the GP, who will make a judgement on the competence of the Service User to make this request.

The Registered Manager must record on the Care Plan that the Service user expressed this wish and record the response of the GP.

However, for legal reasons, we do not operate a Do Not Resuscitate (DNR) policy – it is our strict policy always to resuscitate; what medical professionals do when the Service User has been formally handed into their care is a matter for them.

Euthanasia

If a person in our care commits suicide and you have assisted them in any way at all, this is assisted suicide and you are in serious legal trouble. You are not to do it. Even if the Service User administered the means of death themselves, if you had any involvement at all it is still assisted suicide.

If you administer the means of death for any reason, for example, to “ease their pain”, because the Service User sought and gained your intervention, this is euthanasia and it is illegal.

If a Service User, colleague, other professional, etc. should even as much as hint at your involvement in assisted suicide or euthanasia, etc. you have an obligation to inform the Registered Manager or, if necessary, activate our whistle-blowing policy.

Dying

Responding to Dying

People react differently when they know they are going to die. Some people: deny they are going to die eventually, they become angry and take that anger out on others as denial and anger pass by, reality dawns, they may become depressed □ react badly □ want to talk about it □ bottle it up.

However the person reacts, don't judge – we are all different. Take each situation as it arises and handle it appropriately. Their reactions could include: □ acceptance □ denial □ disbelief □ fear □ guilt □ shock □ worry.

Upsetting others:

Dying people often worry about upsetting those close to them which is why they might talk to us instead of a relative. Naturally, a relative may feel hurt that the Service User spoke to you instead of them. However, you must be professional and respect the trust shown to you by the Service User, even though the relative may be unhappy. If possible, be sensitive and try to help the relative see it from the Service User's point of view.

The Dying Person's Perspective

Having accepted death is inevitable, the Service User might become very sensitive to how people behave towards them, or how they think people are behaving towards them; for example: □ "What will they say to me?" □ "Why haven't they been to see me lately?" □ "Perhaps they won't let me .... anymore?" □ "I don't want to be a burden" □ "I don't want to upset them".

Since these concerns can feel like a heavy weight to the dying person, we have to be careful not to fuel them.

Communication and Dying

When someone is told they are dying, how they react will affect the way they communicate with us and, therefore, how we communicate with them.

For example, someone who accepts they're dying as "the way it is" will communicate with us differently from someone who completely denies it and acts as though nothing has changed.

It might be that they're dying is known to all and an "open" subject, which makes communication reasonably normal.

If they know they are dying but will allow nothing to be said on the matter, this will make us have to think carefully when communicating with them; they are sensitive.

Perhaps we all know the situation and we are avoiding mentioning it as much as they are, so no one says anything – is that right?

Probably the hardest area to deal with is when we know they are dying, and they don't.

Distancing

Not surprisingly, for these reasons, a carer can insulate themselves from the difficulties of communicating with the Service User by not communicating – going through their duties in a way that is almost detached from the Service User.

This is known as distancing and you must avoid it. In care homes, because other people are about, it is more easily spotted and solved than in home care where the carer may be unaware of what is happening – be aware, ask for help!

Making Decisions

The Service User might have decisions to make; for example: □ surgical decisions □ pain relief □ making or changing a will □ dealing with outstanding family issues □ funeral arrangements.

Our ethos encourages the informed decision making of those in our care which means they must: □ have sufficient information □ be competent/assisted to weigh up the issues □ not be manipulated.

Dying may cause their emotional and physical states to change, affecting their ability to make informed decisions. You must not make decisions for them. However, helping them weigh up various options is fine so long as: they specifically ask for your help it genuinely helps them determine what they want to do you do not influence them in any way you keep your manager informed your input is fully recorded in the care plan/personal file.

If you are in any doubt at all, not matter how slight, you must discuss this with your Manager immediately.

Death Approaches …

Check, have we met their needs and recorded them in the care plan, including: emotional needs physical needs spiritual needs medication organ transplant arrangements burial or cremation undertaker Where will they die? How will they die? Who should be at the death? Who do we notify, and how, after the death? Local Authority arrangements.

How will we handle questions like: "Will I be in pain?" "Will I be awake when it happens?" "Will I know it is happening?" "How long will it take?" "Will ….. be here?"

Fear

Question: Are you more fearful of death itself or the way you will die?

This will affect the way we cope with and respond to someone who is dying. As carers, we have to be careful not to let our concerns "rub off" on the Service User, otherwise we have failed to put their needs first.

Fear is a natural feeling related to death, for many reasons. Elderly people, generally, see the reality of death more openly than younger people and have to face those fears in a way they may not have had to when younger.

Some of those more common fears include: □ how I will die □ being a burden □ losing self-control □ pain □ being killed-off.

"How will I Die?"

Since many of us avoid thinking about death or that of someone close to us, we give little thought to "How will I die?" Yet, it is important to think about it to understand the concerns of those we care for because this is one of their most common fears.

There are many ways in which you could die: □ during sleep □ peacefully □ prepared □ privately □ quickly □ slowly □ with/without family □ with/without make up and nails done □ with/without music with/without pain with/without religious involvement to mention but a fear few

Fears

Being concerned about dying is as natural as death itself, some of those fears are perfectly understandable, for example: "How will those left behind cope?" "Will I be frightened when the time comes?" "Who will look after me while I'm dying?"

Some of those fears are more unusual, perfectly real to the Service user, but they may seem odd to us, for example: "What if I come back as a ghost?" "Will they kill me when I'm asleep for my kidneys?" "How will I know I'm dead?" "Who will feed the dog?"

Never tell a Service User their fears are "silly", to them they are definitely not "silly", but very real and worrying.

Acknowledge their fears and discuss them with the Service User rationally and openly. If there is something you or someone else can do to settle their mind, do it.

Symptoms of Dying

The symptoms of dying can become a vicious circle – one symptom can lead to another and another in any ever-decreasing spiral. Symptoms of dying include: pain weakness breathlessness loss of appetite nausea and vomiting constipation water retention confusion.

Pain and Dying

Not everyone experiences pain when dying. However, a slight headache in earlier life, which would have hardly bothered us, might feel a terrible burden when we are dying.

We have to assess, together with the Service User, their pain and their opinion with regards to pain itself. It is not for us to encourage pain relief, which robs the Service User of choice, although we can ask the Service user their opinion – which might change.

You must keep careful records of these discussions, the Service User's views, etc. which must be relayed to healthcare professionals, GPs, etc., to help them fulfil their obligations to the Service User efficiently.

Pain relief could include: drugs taken by mouth injections infusions (drip-fed drugs) complimentary therapies.

Morphine is often used to manage pain and many Service Users can react badly to the suggestion of being given morphine – remember, to them it might signal the end is nigh.

Complimentary therapies used in pain relief could include: acupuncture aromatherapy homeopathy massage music therapy reflexology.

Weakness

As if the weary physical part of weakness isn't bad enough, if the Service User knows they are weak, they know this means they are dying which can cause them emotional distress as well – a vicious circle, again.

Causes of the weaknesses are varied, including: pain frustration loss of appetite.

Their weakness may reduce their mobility which means we have to work with them to avoid pressure sores.

Breathlessness

Breathlessness is a normal part of the dying process, which can be very frightening for the Service User.

To assist them, we could: □ try to help them relax □ consider drugs □ consider oxygen □ use breathing techniques.

Loss of Appetite

Loss of appetite is a very common symptom of dying, which can speed up other symptoms. Reasons for losing appetite could include: □ desire to die □ general loss of interest □ specific illness □ worry.

To help the Service User, we could consider: □ choice of food □ size of meal □ frequency of meals presentation of meals □ discussing weight loss.

Nausea and Vomiting

Nausea is the feeling of wanting to vomit without actually vomiting. Vomiting is bad enough, but the nausea can really wear down someone who is dying.

It is very important that, together with the GP, we get to the cause of the nausea and vomiting in order to find a suitable response.

Tackling the nausea and vomiting can make a huge difference to how the person feels.

Constipation

Most people who are dying suffer from constipation, which can be very upsetting. Just because someone has lost their appetite, does not mean they will not become constipated – they might experience both at the same time.

In most cases, using some form of laxative is normal.

Water Retention

It is usually the arms and legs that retain water when someone is dying, which can become painful, particularly if complicated with skin problems.

The following might help: bandaging exercising

massage.

Confusion

Often, when confusion arises out of the dying process, it can be more of a problem for the relatives or carers than the Service User.

However, if we handle it badly, we could distress the Service user. It is possible the confusion could create triggers for challenging behaviour. Therefore, we must keep accurate and proper records, read and absorb them at shift handovers, etc.

The End is Nigh

At that final point, when the Service user is going to die, their muscles might contract, and it is obvious they have died.

Maybe, their breathing has become erratic and suddenly stopped or perhaps become so shallow it is difficult to determine whether they have died or not.

No two people die exactly in the same way; we are all different.

When it seems apparent they have actually died: □ record the time accurately in their care plan □ close their eyelids □ leave any relatives alone with the deceased □ notify the GP immediately.

DEATH

Immediately After Death

As soon as the person has died, immediately: □ safeguard valuables □ attend to the body □ arrange for the death to be certified.

Safeguarding valuables

Prior to death, arrangements will have been made for safeguarding valuables. These arrangements must be put into immediate effect.

Attending to the body (Last Offices)

Immediately the person has died there are certain brief activities to be performed that must uphold good hygiene practices: remove pillows lie the body straight and flat, on its back insert clean dentures, if worn brush hair

 clean the body, including nails replace any dressings, etc. leave the face uncovered follow any religious, cultural practices.

Certifying the Death

The GP must be called immediately to Certify the Death and, after that, the undertaker, etc. is called.

One hour after the Death: dress the body in clean pyjamas, etc. put a clean sheet under the body put a clean sheet over the body face remains uncovered (follow religious, cultural practices).

Sudden Unexpected Death

It is essential that the most senior person on duty takes charge immediately: do not move the body, leave it where it is (unless it causes distress to others) – particularly if death was due to an accident call the GP immediately where relevant, the GP will call the Coroner who will take charge of the situation.

Removing the Body

Under normal circumstances, the undertaker will remove the body, usually through the front door.

As soon as the body has been removed: strip the bed open windows to air the room fully disinfect the bed replace the mattress, pillows, etc., where necessary.

Registering a Death

If the death is not referred to the Coroner, it must be registered within 5 days. If it has been referred to the Coroner, the Coroner will take charge of the situation.

We will have already located the office to the Registrar of Births and Deaths. The Registrar must be given the Medical Certificate stating the cause of death.

Other useful documents, belonging to the deceased, to give the Registrar include: their medical card their birth certificate their marriage certificate (if relevant).

The Registrar will need to know the deceased's: date and place of birth previous address full names any previous names date and place of death occupation pension details social security details details of living spouse, etc.

When the Registrar is satisfied

When the Registrar is satisfied that all is in order, they will issue either a Certificate for Cremation or an Order for Burial (depending upon which is appropriate) which is given to the undertaker.

Where relevant, a Certificate will be issued for Social Security purposes.

Copies of the Death Certificate issued by the Registrar of Births and Deaths are necessary to satisfy wills, insurances, banks, etc.

Funeral Arrangements

Without a Death Certificate issued by the Registrar of Births and Deaths, no funeral or cremation can take place.

Even then, funeral arrangements cannot be finalised until: the Will is checked for requests financing the funeral is settled.

The undertaker will usually handle matters appropriately.

Funerals and Cremations

For some people, the centuries-old tradition of saying “goodbye” through the funeral or cremation ceremony can bring a sense of freedom, relief, joy. But for others, it can be a sad, numbing, lonely, even devastating experience.

Who Needs Informing?

There are a vast range of organisations that need notifying of a death, which could include: □ cancelling appointments □ Driver and Vehicle Licence Agency □ Financial institutions □ Inland Revenue □ Local Authority □ Passport Office □ Post Office □ Social Security □ Utility providers.

The Benefits’ Agency produce a helpful publication: “What To Do after Death”.

Organ Donation

Without a Medical Certificate issued after death, no organ can be donated. Sometimes, the Coroner’s consent might be required too.

Most organs have to be removed quickly, but some can wait, for example: □ corneas – up to 24 hours after death □ skins – up to 24 hours after death □ bone – up to 36 hours after death □ heart valves - up to 72 hours after death.

If the whole body is being donated, the GP will advise us on what to do

BEREAVEMENT

After the Death

Who will react, in some way or other, after the death? □ you □ colleagues □ other Service Users □ the dead person's relatives □ the dead person's friends.

Handling your own response to the death is one issue, but how will you react to how other people respond to the death?

If you want to cry, cry – go the staff room, office, smoke room, etc., and cry. Tell other colleagues how you feel, talk with them but, please don't "bottle it up".

Reacting to Grief

A typical reaction to someone who is grieving is: "What can I possibly say?" because we are worried of saying the wrong thing.

However, there are definitely two ways in which we can help someone who is grieving, which are: □ practically □ emotionally.

Practical Support

These are the things that you can actually do; for example, putting the bereaved person's bins out, helping them with the shopping, etc.

Emotional Support

Sometimes, just letting the bereaved person know you are there, simply that you are available, can often be enough. If they need more, are willing to accept it and you are willing and able to give it, then, all the better.

Mourning

Not only do we all mourn differently, but different circumstances can affect the way we mourn as well; for example: ☐ our character ☐ mode of death ☐ sense of guilt ☐ things not said ☐ time of death ☐ unfinished business.

Grieving

There are four stages of grieving: ☐ Shock – numbness, can't accept the death ☐ Yearning – pining, grief ☐ Despair – feeling lost, disorganised, depressed ☐ Recovery – life starts to return.

Typically, the initial reaction to death is shock, loss, numbness.

After a few days or even weeks, as the loss sets in, the pain and pining begin to bite. Emotions can vary from anger and guilt through to loneliness and despair, which can go on for many months. Losing control is not uncommon and, sometimes, the intensity of the feelings experienced by the bereaved person can, in themselves, be hard to handle.

Eventually, the bereaved person beings to re-adjust to life without the dead person.

Grieving, helpful hints

Let the bereaved person know you are available □ be prepared to talk about the dead person – they have gone, but the memories haven't □ remember anniversaries □ keep in touch with the bereaved person □ if the bereaved person wants to bring up the dead person in conversation, let them □ don't avoid the bereaved person; they know you are doing it! □ saying you know how they feel might not be quite true; it's not actually helpful!

Chapter 2 Approx. page 72-197

MEDICATION

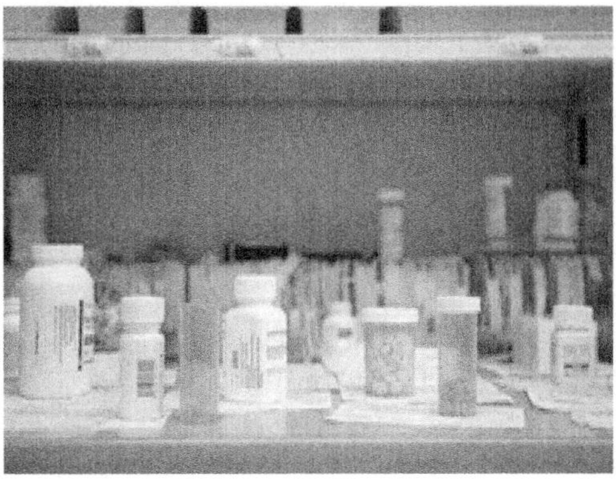

Benefiting from Training

We all have different attitudes to training, we all prefer some topics more than others, we all learn at different rates etc – you know this.

This training source is intended so that having completed it you are both competent and confident in the administration of medication, a responsible role for anyone involved in care work.

Before you start the training, spend a few minutes thinking about medication administration – what would you hope to gain from this material, what might some of your objectives from it be? What some of them down here:

At the end of the training is an evaluation form, compare it with what you have written here – have we met your objectives as well as ours to benefit those we care for?

Purpose

Medication Administration Training is a comprehensive in-house training manual for care providers and suitable for training staff in nursing, residential care, home care, day care etc, in best practices of safe medication administration.

Its purpose is to help those working in care environments develop and maintain competence in the whole process surrounding the safe administration of drugs and medicines through:

Implementing best practice•safeguarding those we care for ensuring accountability •promoting public confidence

The last pages of these resources are a final test sheet, which is a master for you to photocopy and test those trained, together with a summary of worksheets included within this material. Send a copy of those completed final sheets to Head Office so that they can mark and assess them with a view to issuing externally verified Medication Administration training certification.

Introduction

European and North American surveys show that between 40% and 70% of care providers fall short of statutory minimums for the management of drugs and medicines – the scope for serious error is huge.

Medication is a feature of most care provision, some people managing their own needs whilst others having need for the assistance of care workers. Irrespective of the type of care given or its location, the principals of safe drug and medication practices remain the same – duty of care exists throughout every aspect of the medication process.

It is estimated that up to 11% of medications administered, on average, are wrong in some way. This is totally avoidable and completely unacceptable.

This means, being involved in any way with drugs and medication is a responsibility because mistakes can kill.

If you neither feel capable nor are capable of this responsibility you should not be involved with medication, you and your manager need to be clear about this. However, millions of drugs are administered properly every day by people just like you, so, with good training and your commitment, you can do it properly every time too! This training resource is written to help you do just that.

When you get to a worksheet, stop, complete the worksheet and then move on. Do not move on until you have completed the worksheet – They are essential evidence in your demonstrating competence in this vital subject.

Terminology

When it comes to drugs and medication, different people use different words to describe the same thing. For example, going around with the trolley containing the medication is sometimes called a:

Medication round med. Round • medication pass med. Pass

In fact, even the trolley itself has different names:

Medication trolley med. Trolley •medication cart med. Cart

Sources of Information

Obviously, the best place to go for advice or information about medication is your pharmacist and you should develop a good working relationship with the.

Pharmaceutical societies provide lots of information and free fact sheets on most issues you are likely to encounter. Their information can be considered reliable.

Nursing and medical organisations and societies are also reliable sources of information. Be wary of internet information – some of it is good and some of it is not!

Whilst Being make aware;

As you are being trained, you will have to put your initials and date on several documents that are essential in the safe medication process. Checking and signing are vital parts of everything you will do with drugs and medication and if something goes wrong that information could be used in a court – do not let this worry you.

Each step of the way, the person training you will put their initials and date against everything you do. Furthermore, that person will put the letter "T" after their initials and date which indicates they have been training you are accountable for you doing it properly.

Take responsibility – If your trainer has not signed, dated and "T" next to your entries asks them to do so. If they refuse, you are not to continue with the training but must discuss the matter immediately with your manager.

Length of Training

This is one of the most responsible tasks you can be asked to undertake in care work, mistakes can kill.

Therefore, you must take your time and be responsible, a "rush through, sign it off and finish" attitude is not acceptable.

During training, there will be at least

Information to pass on to you • worksheets to complete

evidence of good practice to be demonstrated

•maybe, the need

to do things again • the requirement to demonstrate

competence certification to achieve

Whist there is no formal minimum or maximum training time; it is unlikely you will be able to demonstrate capability in less than 8 hours of training and several times of conducting medication administration under supervision. Up to 12 hours of training and several times of conducting medication administration under supervision is not unreasonable, for some people perhaps loner.

Ideally, break training time into bit sized pieces. A useful way to do this is to take one section of this training resource at a time. Some of the sections might take you 40 minutes, some up to 75 minutes – more or less, we are all different.

This is too important a subject to make mistakes, so, take your time and make sure you understand one section before going on to the next one, because you need to not just know what you are doing but to be able to show that you know it to someone else.

Legislation

Every country has legislation regarding drugs, medication and their administration because it is such an important subject.

Learning legislation word for word is pointless, what matters is how you apply that legislation, what you do with it and this training resource helps you do that.

Essentially, the law makes two groups of people responsible:

- Us, the organisation you work for (employer) • you, the person involved with the medication (employee)

If someone reports to you, you are their employer which means you have the responsibilities of both employer and employee. If you report to someone, you are their employee which means you have the responsibilities of the employee.

Employer's Responsibilities

- Assess risks Tell employees about relevant risks • Provide safe ways of working • Provide safe and suitable equipment (and maintain it) • Train staff • Keep the working environment safe

- Protect anyone not in their employment – clients visitors
- These responsibilities are continuous ongoing – they are not a one off "job done" exercise.

Employee's Responsibilities

- Take care of my own safety •Be careful no-one is harmed by anything I do • Be careful on-one is harmed by anything I didn't do • Co-operate with my employer • Follow written policies/procedures •Work as trained • Don't misuse things
- Tell my employer if I see something potentially harmful, even if danger isn't immediate.

Most errors, dealt with quickly, have minimal consequences – but – some have very serious consequences very quickly, they can kill

If you are accepting the responsibility for medication administration, which can very easily be done properly and well; that is what you have to be – responsible:

Pay attention to what you are doing • take care over what you are doing do not rush check and check again

Hazardous Substances

Exposure to drugs and medications (which are hazardous substances) poses potential risks to anyone involved with those drugs and medications, including you the person administering them.

Providing a safe working environment includes managing risks relating to hazardous substances which include drugs and medication.

Using a following the advice that accompanies medication when it is supplied as part of risk assessment is the start of any good medication management.

Where necessary, we keep a copy of the risk assessment in the Medication on Site Register attached to the relevant information provided by the supplier for that medication. Should a particular medication cause a genuine hazard we will work directly with the pharmacist to manage that risk appropriately.

Thinking About Medication

Before we can learn about the day-to-day do's and don'ts of medication, we need to understand.

What are we dealing with? • Why are we dealing with it?

What is medication? • How does medication work?

How does medication affect us? • How is medication applied?

This helps us appreciate why the do's and don'ts exist which makes us work more safely in the administration of medicines – it is the basis of our being competent.

What is Medication?

Medication is the use of a substance or substances used to treat a health and medical concern. Usually, this involves drugs, but, vitamins and minerals can also be included as medication.

Drugs

Traditionally drugs came from plants and/or herbs – many still do – but chemical processes have taken over, some are even engineered genetically

Some drugs have such mild effects they can be brought from the local shop whilst others have powerful effects and have to be carefully controlled, they may even be illegal. There are drugs that many of us take every day of our normal life – caffeine, nicotine etc

Why Do We Use Medication

Disease control • disease prevention • energy supplements

fighting illness • Health improvement • hormone replacement

mental difficulties • Nutritional benefits• pain relief

physical relief

How Do Drugs Work

Only in the last 75 years have we properly begun to understand how drugs work and there is much we do not know.

Different drugs affect different parts of the body in different ways (and even that can vary between different people) according to:

Dose how much of the drug is use

Frequency how often the drug is used

Some drugs work by:

Improving how certain body cells work, reducing how certain body cells work, affecting hormones in the body, affecting chemicals in the body, altering the messages the body sends to / from the brain

Destroying invading micro-organisms

killing abnormal body cells

How Drugs Affect Us

Whilst drugs are intended to benefit us, because they rely upon altering us in some way, they can harm us as well.

When medication is prescribed (or bought from a shop) a balance has to be found – will the benefit of the drug outweigh the harm it might do?

Some of the effects of drugs could:

- Be almost instant • take a few hours to start • take weeks to get started • Disappear quite quickly • last for days
- have permanent consequences

Our bodies develop and, through time, can adapt and become resistant to the effects of a drug or drugs that might mean a change in medication, increased dose and or frequency.

We are all different – what I respond well to could make you feel ill. This is one reason why when we administer medication we have to be observant. Not just at the time of administering but all the time – how is the client?

That is why we have to understand the effects of people's medication – is it helping them or hindering them?

Adverse Reactions:

These are commonly known as "side effects", the effects that are not good for the person as a result of their medication.

A drug designed to tackle one matter might have an effect somewhere else in their body which could be a cause for concern. We have to know what to look out for and be observant in looking out for it in case it happens.

Interactions

Sometimes, two or more drugs taken together work with each other, they "interact" which can be to the person's wellbeing or it can make them ill. You have to know about these possible interactions and stay observant in case they happen.

The doctor prescribed John medication and you gave John something you bought from the shop for his headache – the two interacted and made John ill.

Whether a medication is prescribed or non-prescription, medication is medication and they can all interact.

The food the client eats, the drink they had, the alcohol they consumed – these can interact with a person's medication too. We need to know about those interactions and stay observant in case they happen.

Oral Medication

Oral medication is the most common way of taking a drug – by mouth – it is swallowed.

The medication passes through the stomach into the intestine where it is broken down, absorbed into the bloodstream and transported to where it will have its effect.

Some medication has to be taken before eating – empty stomach – to get into the intestine more quickly for a quicker reaction.

Other medication has to be taken with or after food to slow its entry into the intestine where its absorption is slower in order for the medication to work properly.

Giving the mediation at the wrong time causes the speed and effectiveness of its absorption into the bloodstream to be wrong. This means the medication will not work effectively which could make the person's condition worse.

Therefore, when we give the medication and what with are extremely important.

Rectal and Vaginal Medication

Some medication is designed to be inserted into the client's bottom – a suppository – in order to enter the bloodstream. This is quite normal where a person has problems swallowing, if they feel nauseous (sick) or are actually vomiting.

Other medications are inserted into the vagina for them to have effect.

Inhaled Medication

Drugs can enter the bloodstream through gases that are inhaled into the lungs, for example, an asthmatic using an inhaler.

Injected Medication

Obviously, medication injected directly into the bloodstream can have a very fast acting effect because it has entered the bloodstream quicker than by being swallowed or via a suppository.

You will sometimes hear the phrase "systemic effect" when drugs are injected directly into the bloodstream.

This simply means the medication has a quick effect on the whole body.

Injections are not just used for having a systemic effect; they can be specifically intended for a particular part of the body.

The three main types of injection are:

Intramuscular	(M)	- directly into muscle
Subcutaneous	(SC)	- under the skin
Intravenous	(IV)	- directly into a vein

Obviously, an IV injection acts quickly because it can get a lot of medication very quickly into the bloodstream.

WARNING

Injections are known as invasive, because they "invade" the body. You must never inject someone under any circumstances unless a) professionally trained by a suitably qualified medical practitioner who has b) given you their written authority to do so under their supervision and c) has assessed you are competent to do so.

Without this, no matter who asks you do no inject.

Topical Medication

These are localised medications that are generally applied to outside parts of the body, they are not to be taken internally, for example:

Creams, ointments, drops, patches

Types of Medication

Oral - Tablet (pill) - Solid usually round, coated drug that is swallowed

Oral – Capsule -Cylindrical shell that, having been swallowed, dissolves slowly to release the drug

Oral - Mixture Dissolve drug/s, usually in water

Oral - Elixir Dissolved drug/s usually in a sweet alcohol/water mix

Oral - Syrup Dissolved drug/s, usually in a liquid syrup

Cream Non-greasy preparation to apply the drug/s to the skin

Ointment Greasy preparation to apply the drug/s to the skin

Suppository Drug/s in a solid bullet shape to enter the vagina

Drops Drug/s in a sterile solution, dropped into the eye, ear, nose

Spray Drug/s in a solution, sprayed into the nose

Inhaler Drug/s in solution under pressure, released in a dose to be inhaled

Medication Policy

You should now read our policies and procedures regarding our medication policy.

Medication is not for social control, reward or punishment –this is an abuse of medication and the person it is being used and / or withheld from. Being involved in such practices is gross misconduct; you will be disciplined and possibly dismissed for gross misconduct. If this has involved abuse, our abuse procedures will apply, and you could be barred from working in care environments.

A supervisor and/or manager “turning a blind eye” to such practices is also culpable and faces similar action.

Section 2 – Drug Groups

Types of Drugs

Analgesics Beta blockers

Antacids

Anti-angina drugs

Anti-anxiety drugs

Anti-arrhythmic drugs

Bronchodilators

Corticosteroids

Diabetic drugs

Diuretics

Anti-cancer drugs
Anti-diarrhoeal drugs
Anti-emetic drugs
Anti-psychotic drugs
Anti-hypertension drugs
Anti-rheumatic drugs
Anti-tuberculosis drugs
Anti-ulcer drugs
Antibiotics
Antihistamines
Antidepressants
Antiseptics
Asthma drugs
HIV/AIDS drugs
Immunosuppressant
Inflammatory bowel drugs
Lipid lowering drugs
Laxatives
Menstrual drugs
Migraine drugs
Muscle relaxants
Sleeping drugs
Vasodilators
Urinary disorder drugs
Vitamins
and others!

Analgesics (painkillers)

Analgesics fight pain, do not tackle the problem causing the pain, therefore, it is still necessary to seek to find out the problem and tackle it.

There are two main groups of analgesics:

Opioids (codeine, methadone, morphine etc) non-opioids (paracetamol, NSAIDSs)

Opioids and paracetamol work on the brain by blocking brain cells from bang able to pass on “pain” messages.

NSAIDs (non-steroidal anti-inflammatory drugs) aspirin, diclofenac, ibuprofen etc – are less powerful than opioids and work by preventing nerve endings at the site of the pain “sensing” the pain.

Antacids:

If the stomach acids become too long and/or the mucous layer that protects the stomach lining is damaged, the stomach acids get to the stomach wall which causes pain. This is often called indigestion. Antacids, being made from alkali, neutralise the acid which relieves the pain.

Anti-angina:

Angina is chest pain caused because blood vessels flowing to the heart muscles have narrowed which reduces oxygen supply to the heart. This could be triggered by stress, physical exertion, fatty deposits in the blood vessels, and muscle spasm in artery walls.

Anti-angina drugs widen the blood vessels which improve blood flow and reduce stress on the heart. Such drugs do not solve the problem, they manage the symptoms.

Whilst quite safe, dizziness and tiredness can be experienced.

Anti-anxiety (tranquillisers):

If certain chemicals in our body imbalance, the person can become anxious to such an extent they can start to show physical symptoms such as shaking, eating difficulties etc.

The types of drugs to deal with this are, broadly, in two categories:

Those that alter brain activity where the anxiety is "felt", for example, benzodiazepines such as diazepam • those that alter the nervous system and organ function to reduce the physical symptoms, for example, beta blockers

Two common problems with benzodiazepines are:

Drowsiness because they are a sedating effect • a shorter useful period because the body begins to get used to, tolerate them

Anti-arrhythmic:

If the electrical impulses that regulate the rhythm of the heart lose their regular pattern, the heart will beat in an irregular rhythm. This is called arrhythmia and is what this type of drug is designed to tackle. There are several different anti-arrhythmic, each aims at

stabilising the rhythm of the heart differently – either on a one-off basis or on a regular
ongoing basis depending upon the person's situation. Usually, the most common problems are dizziness and nausea, but some people can experience visual or breathing difficulties.

Anti-cancer:

The number of anti-cancer drugs keeps growing and there are many new drugs being tested and developed all the time. The all work differently and, in fact, not all of them are full understood. Some of them:

Slow down cell growth • use genetic engineering

"trick" chemical messages

Nausea and vomiting regularly accompany anti-cancer drugs. They nearly all affect the development of blood cells which results in weakness, greater likelihood of infection and reduced ability to fight infections. Most anti-cancer drugs and treatments themselves make the person taking them feel quite ill.

Anti-convulsions:

The electrical signals that move the limbs can mistakenly be sent by the brain in "bursts" which can cause the limbs to jerk, loss of physical control and even loss of consciousness.

These seizures (sometimes called convulsions or fits), for example epilepsy, can be very frightening and dangerous.

Anti-convulsions dampen down the brain's electrical activity to prevent these "bursts" of electrical signals. Unfortunately, this can cause the person taking the medication to feel tired, have difficulty concentrating etc.

Additionally, they affect how the liver breaks down other drugs which can cause other difficulties. Often it takes a while to build up anti-convulsions to the right level for each person needing them. They must be gradually withdrawn which generally occurs two years after the last episode.

Ant-depressants:

Depression is entirely different to the day-to-day "sadness" we can all fell from time to time as life goes by. Depression is a genuine clinical use where because the brain is releasing less chemicals that "excite" us, we become less "stimulated" and, therefore depressed.

It can take up to two weeks before anti-depressants increase the levels of those chemicals where we begin to see their benefit and may have to be taken for months while the brain gets back to normal.

Tolerance can develop; and this has to be carefully managed. Some anti-depressants can cause headache, nausea, vomiting, even heart spasms or fits and certain foods may have to be avoided.

Anti-diarrhoeal:

For many of us, diarrhoea is no more than a brief and unpleasant nuisance. But for some people, it can cause dehydration and/or prevent necessary medication from being properly absorbed.

Anti-diarrhoeal drugs are usually opioids designed to decrease the muscle's "expulsion" activity which helps keep waste matter in the bowel longer. Sometimes, bulking agents are given to help slow down "expulsion" from the bowel.

There is the risk of constipation might occur and even a blocked bowel might arise.

Anti-emetics

Anti-emetics treat the feeling of nausea (wanting to vomit) and/or actual vomiting itself. These are usually symptoms of another problem which should be investigated because anti-emetics are not treating the problem, just its symptoms of nausea and/or vomiting.

These drugs block the signals to the brain that make people feel nauseous or vomitus and, in so doing, stop the person feeling that way.

They can make the person using them have difficulty urinating, feeling drowsy, dizzy – even faint.

Anti-hypertensive

Hypertension is regular high blood pressure that can cause heart attack, stroke, kidney damage and needs treating.

Changes in diet, weight, exercise, lifestyle can help but where they do not, anti-hypertensive drugs may be necessary. As with other drugs, they do not solve the problem but only manage the symptoms of the problem.

Some anti-hypertensive increase the width of blood vessels whilst other reduce the blood volume – both have the effect of reducing the blood pressure.

That blood pressure drop can make people feel dizzy, some may even faint. Sudden withdrawal could rapidly increase blood pressure which could be extremely dangerous.

Ant-psychotics

Some people are described as psychotic where mental problems cause them to struggle with reality, act irrationally etc. Whether this is a short-term problem or a longer term one.

Anti-psychotics (sometimes called major tranquillisers or narcoleptics) reduce the level of chemical (the chemical is called dopamine) transmissions in the brain. Once more, these drugs treat the symptoms of the problem but not the problem itself.

Some anti-psychotics prevent nausea and vomiting so are used before surgery.

Damping down these dopamine transmissions can have a sedative effect. There are long term effects which can cause constant jerking of limbs, face muscles. Withdrawal has to be gradual and managed because otherwise the person can feel very poorly.

Anti-rheumatics

Anti-rheumatics relieve the symptoms of rheumatoid arthritis thereby giving pain belief which boosts the patient's mobility and prevents deformity. How most of these drugs work is not fully understood.

Whilst some of the drugs can become ineffective, others have to be stopped periodically because they have serious side effects.

Anti-ulcer

Antacids can help relieve the symptoms of ulcers, in the stomach and duodenum but do not solve the problem. Unsolved, these ulcers can erode blood vessels leading to a perforated stomach which is serious

Anti-ulcer drugs protect the ulcer form stomach acids which give the ulcer time to heal. Side effects are rare.

Antibiotics

Penicillin, the antibiotic, was only introduced in 1941. Since then, they have been so commonly used that bacteria have become resistant to them hence, for example, the problems with MRSA. (methicillin-resistant staphylococcus aureus. Many animals are routinely fed antibiotics to allow for intensive farming methods, antibiotics, therefore, enter our food chain and we are eating them as food!

There are now many types of antibiotics and they work in different ways, some:

- Kill the bacteria •slow down the growth of the bacteria

- prevent the bacteria developing and making cell walls • damage the chemical structure of bacteria.

A course of antibiotics must be completed, even if the person is feeling better, because, if not, the bacteria may start multiplying again making the person ill, possibly worse than before.

They have few side effects, but, they can kill bacteria which are helpful to us as well as those that are to.

Antihistamines

For treating allergic reactions, these are the most commonly used drugs, and, once more, there are several types.

When the body needs to protect itself from infection it releases a chemical called histamine, a natural body chemical. For some people, the consequence of the side effects of histamine can be very serious. One example of this is anaphylactic shock which causes a rapid drop in blood pressure and is extremely serious.

Antihistamines, as their name suggest, block the effects of histamine which reduces swelling, soreness, redness, watering.

They work in the brain which can result in a sedative effect. Taken with opioids, that sedative effect is greatly increased.

Antiseptics

Bacteria, fungi, circuses can all infect the skin, usually through a wound which can result in infection. Antiseptics (germicides) are chemicals that prevent the invading micro-organisms multiplying and are usually supplied as creams, soaps, ointments etc

Side effects are rare, at worse, minor skin irritation. However, some people can experience an allergic reaction, and this could be serious.

Beta-blockers

The body responds to electrical impulses passed from cells and nerve endings to other cells and nerve endings. Those impulses are passed chemicals called neurotransmitters (some neurotransmitters are hormones instead of chemicals) which "blind" themselves to the receiving cells or nerves at points called receptors.

The receptors that effect our "fight" or "flight" response are called beta-receptors of which there are two types:

Those that effect the heart those that effect the lungs, blood vessels and other body tissue.

When stimulated, these beta-receptors work to pump blood around the body faster and oxygenate it more quickly. Beta-blockers block the impulses that stimulate beta-receptors, which can have a number of effects:

Lowering blood pressure • reducing how hard the heart has to work • relieving migraine • reducing muscle relieving breathing problems

Beta-blockers are widely used to treat angina, hypertension etc. Since they reduce circulation, some people experience cold hands and feet which is a problem for people already suffering from poor circulation.

Sudden withdrawal of beta-blockers can cause a rapid rise of blood pressure which could cause a heart attack.

Bronchodilators

Air enters the lungs through narrow tubes called bronchioles which can become narrower due to muscle contractions or mucous build-up which results in breathlessness.

Bronchodilators do not tackle the cause of the problem, only the symptoms, by relaxing the muscles that allow the bronchioles to widen thereby making breathing more easy. This is usually done by inhalation of the medication.

Since they stimulate part of the nervous system that affects heart rate, they can cause palpitations and, therefore, have to be used carefully if a person has heart problems.

Corticosteroids (steroids):

(Note: These are not the same as anabolic steroids which are different)

They are mainly used to control inflammation by blocking the chemicals that cause inflammation.

Regular side effects are rare but long-term use can suppress the immune system making the risk of infection higher.

If taken for more than one month, the lack of certain hormones could reduce the body's ability to cope with shock which is potentially serious in the case of an emergency.

Diabetes Drugs:

Untreated diabetes results in the narrowing of blood vessels which can result in blindness, kidney failure, reduced circulation, heart attack.

Insulin is an essential hormone in the creation of the body's blood sugar level, which is defective, resulting in diabetes. Anti-diabetic drugs:

Replace the body's own insulin, or, stimulate the body's own insulin production, or alter the rate the body absorbs sugar into the blood.

To be effective, the drugs have to work in partnership with the person's lifestyle – activity levels, food intake, illness etc.

Diuretics:

High blood pressure can sometimes be caused because of too high a blood volume. Body tissue can absorb and hold too much water causing swelling (oedema or oedema).

Diuretics effect how the body reabsorbs water (and sodium) from the kidneys which reduces the water content of the blood and, in so doing, lowers blood volume which reduces blood pressure – this helps the heart work more easily and reduces stress on the heart. Excess water in the body is then used up which reduces swelling.

Urinating becomes more frequent because the body is expelling more water.

Blood chemical and sugar levels can be effected which can cause problems for some people, diabetics, for example.

Immunosuppressant:

Sometimes, it can be necessary to intentionally reduce the body's natural immune system. For example, the immune system would reject a transplant and that would have to be prevented from happening. Some people's immune systems attack their own body – autoimmune disorder – requiring the immune system to be suppressed.

Since such drugs suppress the body's immune system, there can be potentially serious side effects such as reduced ability to fight infection, kidney damage, brain damage.

Inflammatory Bowel Disease (IBD)

Inflammation of the intestinal wall creates stomach pain, feeling ill, diarrhoea, loss of appetite, weight loss – Crohans disease is an example.

Currently, drugs do not cure the problem but control the symptoms and prevent complications by relieving the inflammation which gives the intestine time to recover.

The nature of the problem often requires the use of suppositories.

Side effects of the drug used can be serious which requires regular blood testing to monitor the situation.

Laxatives

Fibre in the diet makes faeces soft, so a lack of fibre can result in constipation. High fibre diets and drinking plenty of water often helps prevent constipation. Lack of exercise, being bed ridden can also increase the likelihood of constipation which is why care providers have to appreciate the problem and seek to prevent it.

Laxatives are generally in two forms:

Bulking agents, stimulants

Bulking agents increase the bulk of bowel movements which make expulsion more likely.

Stimulants increase contractions of intestine muscles; they absorb less fluid which makes the faeces more fluid and expulsion more likely.

If laxatives are used too regularly, the bowel can become lazy and dependence can arise.

Lipid Lowering:

Too much body fat (lipid) can restrict blood flow and/or cause clots which increases the likelihood of heart attack, stroke.

When diet and lifestyle changes have not worked, lipid lowering drugs might be necessary. They do not solve the problem but reduce lipid (fat) levels – mainly cholesterol – in the body.

Vitamin supplements might be necessary and people with kidney or liver problems could find those problems made worse by lipid lowering medication.

Menstrual Disorders:

Most drugs to treat menstrual disorders are hormonally based – oestrogen, progestogen – and their uses include:

Pain relief, blood flow reduction, premenstrual syndrome relief

Controlling menstrual regularity

Migraine

Migraine, a severe usually recurrent headache, is due to changes in blood vessels around the brain. It can cause/be accompanied by nausea, vomiting, numbness, tingling, "flashing" lights and can be very disabling, yet, no one really knows why it happens.

Learning to identify what triggers an attack helps prevent and/or reduce the impact of an attack. Sometimes an analgesic helps, other times more specific medication.

Migraine medication seeks to reduce the pain causing chemicals and/or alter the "feeling" of pain, essentially "tricking" the brain to thinking there is no pain.

Drowsiness is the most common side effect, but regular use of certain migraine drugs can damage blood vessels and even result in dependence.

Muscle Relaxants:

Muscle relaxants can work either by:

Directly on the muscle, reducing messages sent to the brain

They treat muscle spasm which is causing the muscle to tighten or stiffen by relaxing the muscle which improves mobility.

Too high a dose can cause weakness and long term; the body can develop dependence.

NSAIDs (non-steroidal anti-amatory drugs):

Certain chemicals produced when there is an injury cause inflammation and, subsequently, pain.

Reducing the inflammation reduces both the pain and any stiffness – that is what NSAIDs do. Therefore, they have many uses, including:

Arthritis, back pain, menstrual, pain, rheumatism Sprains, strains. They are quite safe but, occasionally, can cause stomach bleeding. Anyone with kidney or liver problems is more at risk of NSAID side effects.

Sleeping Medication (hypnotics):

Their intent is to help re-establish a good sleeping pattern not to “do the sleeping” for the person they have been prescribed to.

By disturbing nerve cell communication, the brain thinks there is less going on and reduces its activity helping the person fall asleep. The sleep is not the same as normal sleep; it is not the “resting” sleep the body needs to feel refreshed which is contributory to the increased risk of drowsiness and falling.

On withdrawal, the person naturally returns to normal sleep where dreams occur which, initially, can seem more vivid because the person has not been so used to dreaming. This might result in restlessness; even fear of sleeping which requires sleeping medication to be re-introduced, a vicious cycle can develop.

Stimulants:

Some brain chemicals increase awareness, they "stimulate" us. Without them working properly, we may become sleepy, have difficulty staying alert etc.

These drugs stimulate the brain which increases our alertness and include caffeine, a natural stimulant.

Stimulants can take over our brain's natural stimulants leading to dependence requiring careful withdrawal, loss of consciousness could happen. Too much stimulant harms sleep, causes nervousness. In severe cases, hallucinations can be stimulated which is why some people take them illegally – amphetamines.

Vasodilators:

Improve blood supply by relaxing muscles surrounding blood vessels allowing them to widen thereby increasing blood flow.

Often used to reduce blood pressure and relieve stress on the heart. Headache, dizziness, fainting are the more common problems associated with vasodilators.

Vitamins

Easily provided through a well-balanced diet, particularly fresh fruit and vegetables. Children, the sick, certain conditions, the elderly are more at risk from vitamin deficiencies and their consequences.

Non-prescription Medication

There are several different names for non-prescription medication, the medication you can buy legally without prescription, those names include:

Household remedies, homely remedies domestic medication. Over-the-counter medication

Every client has the right to buy these medications (for headaches, colds etc), whether it is in their best interests or not, and we must not impair that right.

We can, of course, seek to inform them where otherwise they may not be making a fully informed decision, but, informing is not influencing or manipulating them. That informing may require us to take advice form a pharmacist regarding possible interactions between prescribed medication and that which is not prescribed, however, only for the purpose of supporting the client make informed decisions.

These medications are still drugs; you may not administer them unless:

Trained in medication administration, authorised to administer medications all our medication procedures are satisfied all our recording procedures are in place and satisfied we have formal consent from the client

Possible consent difficulties should be discussed with the client, family, representative, advocate, health and social care professional etc. in advance and agreements and actions recorded in the care plan.

Drugs and Clients

At Risk Groups

There are certain groups of people that are more at risk from the side effects of medication, these groups include:

Infants children pregnant women elderly people with kidney or liver damage those on long term medication

Infants and Children

Are more at risk because their:

Body composition is different to adults body water levels are higher which reduces drug concentration kidneys are less able to excrete drugs

Liver is less able to break drugs down

Pregnant Women:

Are more at risk because of:

Adverse development of the foetus • low birth weight

Miscarriage • Premature birth

Breast feeding can transfer small molecules of drug form the mother to the baby via the milk which can affect the baby.

Elderly Persons:

Are more at risk because they:

Experience physical changes due to ageing • are more likely to have drugs build up in their body more regularly use larger doses of drugs • Experience increased sensitivity to drug effects • change as to how their bodies absorb drugs

change as to how their bodies excrete drugs

Can experience irregular treatment – forgetting, missing, double-dosing etc

Kidney and Liver Problems:

People with kidney or liver problems are more at risk because their:

Kidneys do not excrete drugs properly livers do not break drugs down properly drug levels build up in their body, bodies have too much active drug in the body

Know Your Medications

If a client asked you basic information about their medication you should be able to answer them on these basic points:

What it is for what it does its normal dose

possible side-effects contraindications precautions

**contraindications are those about the client that could increase the risk of an adverse effect – their current situation, medical history etc*

You are not expected to become a walking medical reference book, but, if you could not answer these basic questions when administering a medication, why are you administering it?

If more information beyond this is required, have the most senior person on duty liaise with the pharmacist for the information to be provided.

Why not produce a summary list, obviously maintaining client confidentiality that would provide you with already -reckoner reference for these points that could be kept in the med. Cart?

To help you with this, you will need a formulary which is a book listing various drugs, their uses, side effects etc. If we do not have an up to date one we can ask our pharmacist which is the best to use and where to get it form

Medical Register

Every client should have a medication register kept on their care plan which should include the following: The purpose of the medication the prescribed dosage the prescribed frequency how it is to be taken eating and drinking instructions adverse effects risks special precautions Observed interactions observed allergies

Giving Advice

Under no circumstances – no matter how helpful you are trying to be – must you never give advice about medication.

Respond to people's questions by telling them what the patient information leaflet, formulary, pharmacist etc. says but do not give advice; have you been professionally trained as a pharmacist?

If the response to the question, based on the above, has not answered the client's request satisfactorily, that information will have to be given to them by the pharmacist and/or doctor directly.

Contraindications

All of us are made differently with various medical histories and levels of health which could increase or decrease the likelihood of us being adversely affected by a particular medication or medications.

A contraindication is some factor within that which increases the likelihood of us experiencing an adverse reaction from a particular drug or drugs.

Generally, where there is a clear contraindication it does not cause too much of a problem, but, some contraindications can be serious, even life threatening.

Therefore, if a client shows an adverse effect – even if you think it is not the medication – notify the most senior person on duty immediately. They will have the doctor contacted urgently who will take charge of the situation and advise what to do next.

In addition, the episode should be recorded in the client's care plan and a note made on their medication administration record.

Adverse Effects

If you suspect – whether you are sue or not does not matter – that a person has been affected adversely by a medication, notify the most senior person on duty immediately.

They will have the prescriber (doctor) contacted urgently in order to follow their advice. The episode must be recorded in the client's care plan and a note made on their medication administration record.

Allergies

If there are known allergies, these must be explained by a person prescribing medication when they are prescribing it because that allergy and medication may cause adverse effects.

A record must be entered into the client's care plan that this information was given to the prescriber. It is good practice to keep a record of allergies in the person's care plan anyway.

It is good practice to mention the allergy situation when a repeat prescription is requested because a different supplier for the same medication could have different ingredients in the medication that could themselves create adverse effects better safe than sorry!

Drug Tolerance

Our bodies can adapt to the effects of medication, they can become tolerant to it. Becoming tolerant is not the same as dependence which is explained next.

Tolerance reduces the effect of the medication which could result in having to:

Either increase the dose • and/or increase the frequency

In turn, this could lead to tolerance at a higher level, and so it goes on. Sometimes, for example tolerance to alcohol and other medication, combined tolerances can create difficult complications.

Dependence

This is where the substance has become irresistible to the user, which puts them at risk from harm. They "have to" use the substance, despite the harm, because they have become dependent upon it, addicted to it

Dependence could be either:

Psychological physical

Psychological Dependence:

The user thinks has become convinced, they are better off with the substance and that not having it would be unhelpful to them.

Physical Dependence:

The body physically “needs” the substance and not having it causes genuine and sever physical pain – withdrawal symptoms.

Dependence can be upon many substances, for example:

Caffeine - stimulant nicotine, stimulant sleeping drugs;

Alcohol, depressant, barbiturates, anti-anxiety stimulants cocaine, amphetamine

Medication Reviews

Understandably, ensuring medication is working as intended and to manage the problems of tolerance and dependence, it is good medication management to review the medication clients are taking. Particularly if the client is taking medication/s on a long-term basis.

The needs of the client, the type of medication etc. will ultimately determine how frequently medication should be reviewed.

However, every client should have their medication formally reviewed with their medical practitioner at least annually. If the person is taking four or more medications, that review should be at least every six months.

The review should include:

Reason for medication type of medication type of client, Age of client, health of client, reaction to treatment, adverse effects, benefits achieved continuing suitability of medication

Clients New to Our Service

Across a range of issues, anyone new to our care provision should enjoy as smooth a transition into our care as possible which must have involved careful planning in advance.

Their medication regime is an essential part of this which is why we must know what medication they use, why it is used etc. before we take over responsibility for their care provision. This includes making sure there is sufficient supply for their needs during the transition period.

The moment we take on their care provision we must check their medication:

Is it in date? is it correctly labelled? is it the right medication for this person? the same checks we would make as if we were administering it

Client Leaving the Care home

There could be several reasons why someone leaves our care provision including moving to a different area, change of circumstances, change in needs, change in health, death etc

If they are moving from our care to somewhere else we need to ensure their medication is sufficient in supply for the transition period, correctly labelled and that where they are going to is suitably informed to take over their medication needs safely.

Should someone die, we must keep their medication for at least seven days in case there is an inquest into their death.

After someone leaves our care, medication records must be kept for at least three years after the last entry and kept in a safe place where confidentiality is maintained.

Children's records must be kept for at least fifteen years after the last entry and kept in a safe place where confidentiality is maintained.

Before Drug Administration

Any and every aspect of medication with regards to a client requires consent. The medication prescribed to someone belongs to them, it is their property, and therefore, the use of that medication is their business – requiring consent.

Consent can only be given if the person has made a fully informed decision as to what they are giving consent to and why. That is why, where for legitimate reasons, a person genuine inability to give consent is may be given by relatives, representatives, advocates etc.

Authorised Persons

We keep and review a list of persons that are authorised to administer medication, they have been:

- Properly trained • assessed as competent • supervised administering medications within the last 12 months • shown to have retained their competency • able to demonstrate delivery of our medication management system

If you are not on that list you are not authorised and must not engage in the administration of medication in any way at all – no matter who asks you to.

Breach of this is a disciplinary matter for you and the person, if any, that had been involved in you breaching this. The list is on display where anyone can see it so that there is no confusion.

Medication Keys

Keys that provide access to medication trolleys, storage areas etc. have to be taken great care of.

They should only be handled by persons authorised to partake in medication administration and then only when needed for a task directly involving medication management and must be kept on the person in charge at all times.

A "master" medication key (or set of keys) is kept in a safe locked restricted place accessible only by the most senior person on duty. The most senior person on duty keeps the medication key/s that are to be used on a day-to-day basis on their person at all times, changing hands at shift handover to the incoming most senior person on duty.

Record Keeping

Every record related and involved in medication administration and medication management must always be written:

In BLACK ink legibly, so that it can be read by the person that did the task, not someone on their behalf at the time the task happened. And supported by the date and your initials

If medication is refused and/or a dose missed etc. this must be entered in red ink dated and initialled by you in red.

Some people treat records relating to drugs that are not controlled differently to those that are controlled – we do not. We expect the same best practice standards

to apply to record keeping no matter what medication is involved.

Recording Refused Medication

On the medication administration record (we will look at this later during the training programme) you will:

Put a RED circle on the sheet put your initials in RED along with the date you will put an "R" in RED, next to the entry to show it was refused

This is not the only way to identify a refusal, but it is the best way and means we are all doing the same thing which reduces error.

Pharmacy Records

Pharmacy records and documents have to be clear and accurate because the pharmacist is responsible for the consequences of error and/or misunderstanding. They might keep records regarding certain categories, types, quantities of medication dispensed. If you want to know more, arrange to meet our pharmacist.

Prescriptions

Reading a prescription can be difficult because of:

Medical shorthand being used poor handwriting poor eyesight Reading difficulties But, a client must know what is being prescribed and why:

The dose, the frequency the method oral etc)

possible side effects with or without food etc

If the client is unable to collect their prescription when it has been made up the pharmacy will want your signature, if you have been authorised to collect it. They might as for your ID, please, respect their being cautious.

For your benefit, our, the pharmacist, the client – only use original prescriptions. Do not use faxed prescriptions or e-mail prescription "arrangements" because if anything goes wrong we could all be in serious trouble – original documents only!

Authorisation to Change Medication

Never accept a verbal instruction to change any medication, no matter who asks you to whether that is a: Supervisor , manager, nurse, doctor pharmacist

Anyone else

If you act on a verbal instruction and something goes wrong, what evidence do you have that anyone asked you, therefore, who is in trouble then?

Only act upon an order to change medication where that order is by a person authorised to prescribe medication, in writing and stating:

The name of the client the address of the client what it is being changed from what it is being changed to why it is being changed When to start the change dose

frequency method to be taken by name, address and telephone number of people authorising the change Date, their signature

A "squiggle" from them on the medication administration record or care plan is not good enough because it does not provide us with the information to administer that medication safely and professionally.

We might consider accepting a fax change so long as it satisfies the above and we know it will be confirmed in writing on an original document within 7 days of the fax. The decision maker for this is the most senior person on duty at the time of the change.

Labels

Understandably, labels and medication are exceedingly important.

They must NEVER be altered or changed in any way at all and certainly not to be removed.

If there is a label error:

do not use that medication

notify the most senior person on duty immediately

record the problem on the medication administration record

The most senior person on duty will contact the pharmacist

the pharmacist will advise what to do that advice will be recorded both on the care plan and the medication administration record that advice will be followed

Presentation

This refers to the way in which medication has been packaged in preparation for use, how it is presented.

It is best that any solid dose should be kept in a child resistant container, to prevent accidental use. Sometimes, this may not be appropriate, for example, the client cannot open their medication (although there are aids to solve this).

Several medications are supplied to the pharmacist in the way they are to be presented to the client. Some are not and the pharmacist makes them up as they are to be presented.

Supplying Medication

The law controls and regulates the supply of medicines, usually; there are three main categories of supply:

that which any shop can sell • that which a qualified pharmacist can sell

That which can only be supplied if a written prescription has been made by a suitably qualified person.

Who Owns the Medication?

This is very simple, the person to whom the medication is prescribed, supplied to, is the owner of that medication – it is their property.

If you give that medication to another person, which you should not do anyway, you have supplied medication to someone for whom it was not meant – what could the consequences of that be for them, us and you?

If two people in our care are prescribed the same medication, you only give the medication to the person named on the label – you do not give John's medication to Marie, even though it is the same medication. Medication is not a stock for you to select form.

Would you give Marie the slippers that belonged to John – so why their medication? This applies whether the medication is:

Prescribed non-prescription eye, ear drops etc nutritional supplement etc

Medication Receipt

We could receive medication from one or more of several sources which could include:

Pharmacy doctors bag hospital, previous care provider

The client friend, family, visitor etc

No matter how it is received, we must know about it and manage it properly. At any time, we have to know what medication a client has legitimate access to, and we should have a medication record to support that.

Allowing for the client's rights, we must establish upon receipt of a medication, what it is for, dose, frequency, side effects etc from an authoritative source.

We should establish and create a medication received record:

Clients name name of medication who prescribed it their address and telephone contact date of receipt strength of medication dose, frequency, quantity received, expiry date

Self-administering we are administering and risk assessment.

Medication – Stock Management

In the same way you would use the soup you bought last week from the supermarket before the soup you bought this week (stock rotation), so too for medication.

Always check medication dates and use current supply before a new supply so long as the current supply has not reached or past its expiry date.

Stock Checks

In large care facilities, regular medication stock checks are essential to ensure good medication management – maybe even monthly or quarterly.

In smaller care facilities, an annual audit and check is important. If you have a lot of medication for different people you might consider doing these six monthlies.

Remember, two people should do this together and both should be on the current and up to date appointed medication person's list.

Storage

With the exception of controlled drugs, a secure locked cupboard is satisfactory for most medication. However, a dedicated and locked "clinical" store is far preferable, and some inspectors insist on this to increase the security of medications where they feel it is appropriate.

That storage must be:

Secure and kept locked at all times

designated specifically for medication and clinical storage

suitably equipped for purpose, you should be able to see every label

of a suitable sized to be used for its purpose

off the floor

Well organised, tidy and everything put away

below 25◦C

Well-lit

out of direct sunlight

No medications (prescription or non-prescription) should ever be stored in:

Bathrooms (humidity can impair them)

toilets

kitchens

Communal areas

first aid boxes

plastic tubs in the manager's office, etc

Naturally, a person living at home can keep their medication wherever they like, but, educating them with regard to the above is ultimately better for the client.

Underestimating the Size

The majority of medication audits reveal how often care providers underestimate the size of space genuinely needed to store medication properly, think about:

Ostomy products

dressings

sharps

sharps disposal

Nutritional supplements (these are not to be stored in the kitchen)

Incontinence aids

any "medical" items

gloves aprons

Any "clinical" items

any "nursing items

the various medication registers

medication trolley when not in use, refrigerator for cold store medication, bulky MDS trays

Suddenly, one shelf in the manager's office with all the pills and potions stuffed onto it does not seem quite right!

Security:

Not only must the storage area/s be secure when not in sue, they must also be secure during times when they are in use – new supplies, starting a med. Round, finishing one etc. Being locked at all times is a mandatory necessity.

Homecare- Medicine Cabinets

We cannot tell clients where to put their medication, but, with good intent we can responsibly look to educate and inform – not force or bully!

Most medicine cabinets are in bathrooms where humidity can damage medication other problems include:

Size to small, access – not always good lighting cannot always see what they are taking cluttered toothbrushes, tea, coffee etc

Material – not metal and strong security, probably cannot be locked at all risk can easily be broken into

Even less acceptable is the use of such cabinets in care homes, even small "family style" units for the same reasons and breach of duty of care issues.

Refrigeration – Cold Storage

Many medicines are required to be kept at low temperatures, for example, Insulin.

Medicines that require cold storage, refrigeration must be only ever kept in a refrigerator specifically for medication only.

Medication never goes into a food refrigerator

food, drink etc never go into a medication refrigerator

The medication refrigerator is kept in the same place where every other medication is kept so its security is as assured as every other medication.

Just like the food refrigerator, the medication refrigerator has its temperatures checked and recorded daily. Any problems should be reported to the most senior person on duty immediately who will take appropriate action.

There must be a cleaning schedule that determines in advance when the medication fridge when will be cleaned and defrosted.

Drug Administration

Everything is this training resource is essential to good medication administration and you should ensure you feel confident that you have understood.

If not, be honest with yourself and your trainer. It is better to recap something now and understand it properly. If you do, you will get maximum benefit from section 5 because this is where you are going to commence the practical part of the medication administration.

This is the section where you need to:

Concentrate – think about what you are doing and why take your time – mistakes take longer!, Don't rush – mistakes take longer!, Check what you are doing do not feel awkward asking for help

Remember:

Thousands of people, just like you, have had to learn how to administer medication properly and if they can do it successfully without making mistakes, so can you!

Advance Preparation

Sometimes, a trained person will prepare medication for an untrained person to administer it later. For example, someone on an evening shift "makes up" for an untrained night colleague.

This is totally unacceptable – an untrained person is going to administer medication. Every shift where medication is going to have to be administered has to have a suitably properly trained person, there is no alternative option.

Note, however, some medications are intentionally prepared in advance, insulin preparations can be an example but that is a different matter.

Advance preparation is one of the most common causes of error and it must not happen.

Infection Control

For infection to spread it needs:

A source a host, means of transmission

Obviously, when administering medication, all three exist and the best practices of infection control must apply.

You should not consider administering medication unless you have been trained in infection control and are able to demonstrate such that will include:

Proper hand washing techniques cleanliness of equipment, application of UICPs

If you do not know what UICPs are, you need training in infection control and your manager needs to arrange this.

When you are busy, it is easy to be tempted to rush a medication round, particularly not washing your hands and/or not changing your gloves. The most important aspect of infection control with regard to medication administration is breading the chain of infection – removing the means of transmission.

Wash your hands before you start the round, wash them after administering to each client (or, change your gloves properly).

This is not to slow you down or make your life difficult but necessary practical precautions in the fight against infection; they are part of medication administration.

Medication Trolley (Cart)

The medication trolley (med, trolley, medication cart, med. Cart) is the usual means of transporting medication from where it is stored, around a building, floor etc. to administer medication from, before being returned to its storage point at the end of the med.

Round. It is one of the most, if not the most, important piece of equipment used in medication administration.

It Should Be:

Ideally, made of a solid metal construction

designed so the wheels allow the trolley to move easily over carpet, where necessary

fitted with a strong secure, reliable and working locking mechanism

fit for purpose, not just good at some of the task well organised, neat and tidy, clean and tidy

You can see from the instruction on the following page, a good trolley to administer medication properly has to be capable of undertaking many functions with the storage capacity and space to do them.

Using the Medication Trolley (Cart)

When in Use:

A summary of medications to be used and their side effects etc. Should be on the med. Cart for each med. Pass.

It must be equipped with a suitable number of medication cups

There should be at least one med. Cup per client

The clean ones, not yet used, should be stacked hygienically upside down

The used ones should be stored away from everything else where they cannot cross-contaminate anything

A supply of clean, hygienic medication spoons should be available, one for every liquid medication

Fruit juices, water etc should be fresh for each med. Round and kept in covered jugs

A sharps bin should be kept safely on the med. Cart where it cannot cross contaminate (where sharps are going to be part of the med. round)

Non-clinical waste should be suitably hygienically disposed of on the trolley

Clinical waste should be suitably hygienically disposed of on the trolley

A safe container that cannot be tampered with should contain refused medication

The person administering opens the cart for each administration and locks it whilst administering

The trolley stays locked when not in use

Security is essential

The person administering keeps the keys on their person at all times – never left hanging in the trolley door.

Clean gloves and aprons should be on the trolley.

The medication administration records should be accessible whilst maintaining confidentiality working black and red ink pens

The tablet cutter should be clean and hygienic

Never should any medication be left on the trolley in case it is taken by someone

Interruptions and Distractions

Every medication pass has interruptions and distractions, you can almost guarantee it! These are consistently one of the main sources of error and you have to prevent that.

It may be hard, but you are going to have to exercise self-discipline and assertiveness, you have to stop interruptions and put aside distractions.

When someone interrupts you, politely guide them to leave you alone and, where necessary promise to get back to them later – make a note so you do not forget! – or find someone who is passing by to sort the matter out for you.

Only in a genuine emergency can you interrupt a medication round – secure the trolley first – this will happen naturally if you are in the habit of doing it properly.

Medication Administration Timing

For a start, to make this more straightforward, there should be a ready reckoner that briefly lists which clients need which medication and when:

Unless specified elsewhere, and with good reason, good medication practice means medication is administered:

No more than 30 minutes early no more than 30 minutes late

Typically, this creates a one-hour window to accurately medicate and could mean more than one person having to administer from separate medication trolleys to prevent confusion – this needs planning and preparation by the most senior person on duty.

Remember, medication is for the benefit of those we care for which means medication rounds are not for our convenience but for the client.

This also means being sensitive to what is going on around medication. No wonder Marie did not eat her lunch with a nose full of drops 5 minutes before she went to have her lunch and felt very uncomfortable.

Labelling

NEVER administer a medication unless:

The label is clear, the label is printed, the label is easy to read, it is clear who supplied the medication there is not confusion

If multiple containers are supplied, each container must be properly labelled so the above can be determined, you learned about label errors on page 98. The next page provides more details regarding what a label should say.

With monitored dosage systems (you will earn about these in section 8) each separate supply must be correctly labelled. If not, do not administer, notify the most senior person on duty who will contact the pharmacy for instruction.

Where you encounter a label problem, record this on the medication administration record in black ink with your initials and date it.

Never alter a label, even if you intent were to make something more clearly. A faulty label is a faulty label and it has to be put right properly. Sadly, you will get no thanks if your good intention goes wrong.

The minimum information that must be on a label is:

The client's name the name of the medication the strength of the medication the dose to be taken the frequency to be taken

The method to be taken by – oral, rectal etc the date of supply

The name of the supplier, pharmacist etc the address of the supplier

The telephone number of the supplier

If anything of this is missing or in any way not clear, DO NOT administer

Wherever you encounter a label problem:

Make a record of it in black ink on the medication administration record

Notify the most senior person on duty they will contact the pharmacy for instruction that advice will be recorded that advice will be followed

Medication Calculations

Nowadays, it is becoming more and rarer for most care facilities to have to make calculations for administering the correct dose etc. because so much of the medication we receive is already provided in a manner ready for use. However, if you do have to make calculations:

Ensure the pharmacists advice is in writing follow those instructions carefully .Double check your calculations

if you are unsure, have another person check it with/for you

NEVER FORGET, it takes a lot loner putting a problem right than getting a second opinion in the first place – think smart work smart!

Computerised Administration Records

More medication administration records are becoming computerised and there are some highly technical ways of doing it. But, they are only as good as the accuracy and care you give to filling in/keying in the information.

If you are going to be using computerised medication records:

Follow the suppliers instructions to the letter

accuracy standards are just as high as manual records

a backup of the records must be taken at a set time every day

that back up must be timed and dated that back up must be initialled by the person that generated it and must be locked away immediately in a fire proof safe those records must be kept for three years (seven for children's records)

Manual Administration Records

The records kept for the actual administration of a medication to a client are the most important documents to do with medication and have to be treated with respect.

Important Terminology

They are known as the Medication Administration Record which is commonly abbreviated to the letters MAR. We will use these letters MAR form now on every time colleagues refer to them as the "MAR sheets", it is another way of saying the same thing.

Computerised medication administration systems also rely on MAR sheets, but, some more sophisticated systems have handheld computers for entering the details and downloading them when you have finished the medication round

The next page gives you a blank example of a typical MAR sheet although there are lots of variations used.

Medication Administration

Once more, prescription medicines are only administered to the person they were prescribed to, they are their property. Sometimes, the client will come to a specific place at the set time for their medication. If this is the case, where they are administered must be:

Able to administer immediately with the MAR available immediately, Secure, capable of being locked in an emergency

However, excepting home care and self-medication, most care facilities take the medication to the client, usually via a medicine trolley. Taking medication to people made up and put into medication cups on a dining tray is not professionally good practice and falls short of security, hygiene, disposal, documentation, confidentiality standards etc.

Care practices require that we administer medications in ways that uphold the client's:

Dignity, independence, privacy

You, as the person administering the medication, have a specific personal responsibility that the medication is administered correctly and as it should be without error. Do it NO OTHER WAY no matter who says so or why. If anything at all during the medication administration process is not right, then:

stop now!, security – lock up the trolley, storage area etc

Record the concern on the MAR. notify the most senior person on duty immediately for advice.

Record Keeping and MAR (Medication Administration Record) Sheets

Inspections and surveys are often critical of the poor record keeping standards of MAR sheets. This is important, for example, if something went wrong and the record could not be understood, even though you had done your work properly, how could you prove it? Remember, the MAR is a legal evidence document, use it properly.

The MAR must be:

Able to be clearly read, accurate factual completed at the time of administration identifiable – who completed it – your initials, Dated time

Anyone looking at or auditing the MAR must be:

Able to read it understand it, see what is going on

See when it went on see who did it, in case of need for clarification

If the MAR does not satisfy these standards then action must be taken by the manager to put that right, this is non-negotiable – MAR sheets have to be right.

Stage 1 – Administration

Check the Label:

This is NOT a casual glance at the label, it is a genuine check, and you have to pay attention. Becoming familiar with the same routine, same faces, same drugs, same environment, same paperwork, same interruptions, and same distractions does not help, but, you must pay attention – mistakes can kill.

You expected to read “John” on the label because you have done it so often, you have not really concentrated, merely thought you saw “John” on the label and gave him the drugs. As you entered it on the MAR you realised, too late, the medication you have given John was for Jean – now what are the implications?

As you check the label, stay alert, is it:

The right person, the right medication, the right strength

The right dose, the right frequency the right time

Within date, not expired. following specific instructions – food, drink, other etc

If anything is not right stop now, record it in the MAR, lock everything up securely, summon the most senior person on duty who will take charge of what to do next.

Stage 2Administration

You are genuinely satisfied that everything about the label and the MAR is right and it all tallies, we are ready to proceed.

Administration of the Medicine

Check – look at the client, is this the right medication / right client?

Would a picture on the MAR have helped?, are your hands clean and/or gloves on?, the medication goes into a clean medication cup do not touch the inside of the med. Cup in case you cross contaminate it

Place the medicine container (medicine. Cap) on top of the medicine trolley, put the medication back into the trolley, lock it – keep the keys, not left in the door go to the client with the medication in the medicine. Cap ask them, are they ready for their medication – you need consent, (for now, we will work on the basis they take the medication)

Stage 3 – Observation

The purpose of medication, despite what some care workers might think, is not "quick in, quick out" it is a personal professional responsibility. Therefore, observe, you have to see the client physically take their medication and, if it is oral, swallow it.

Do not rush them, you might have to talk them through swallowing it – at their pace. Do not badger and bully, “hurry up, Anna, I am busy” – you being busy is your problem, not theirs!

Unless the person is self-medicating (in which case, why are you administering to them anyway?) never leave their medication with them to take it later, even if they ask you to. How could you be sure they actually took it; you never saw them take it, did you?

If they are not going to take it, for whatever reason, that is their choice. Remove it, place it in the container for disposal and record the refusal properly, in the MAR. This will be reported to the most senior person on duty at the end of the medicine round who will take charge of the situation from there

During the observation you have an opportunity to assess the client:

Changes in them before their medication? changes in them after their medication, how do they seem generally?

Before starting stages 1, 2 and 3 for the next client – gloves off, hands washed, new gloves. Infection control starts with you and it is a part of medication administration NOT an additional “would be nice if I had time”.

Stage 4 – MAR (Medication Administration Record)

Assuming the medication went as it should, which in most situations is normally the case:

Enter the dose taken how it was taken – oral, rectal, drop etc identify the time it was taken your initials any notes necessary Any observations on their conditions • any adverse effects Any contra-indications any reason to withhold medication That it was refused, recording this correctly if undergoing training your trainer will a) countersign b) date

c) put the letter "T" next to entry

These entries onto the MAR are entered now, before the next client, not:

Three hours later after the medicine round after your break by someone else on your behalf – but by you and you only

Stage 5 – Round Completed

Having made the trolley secures and locked it away properly

Dispose of waste bag properly dispose of clinical waste bag properly Drug waste and/or refusals to be stored appropriately to be returned to the pharmacist for destruction subject to use by controls, any surplus fruit juices etc. labelled and into anon-clinical fridge for storage, check the sharps container, if it is 75% full it is ready for collection for disposal Medication, spoon, medicine cup etc. stocks suitable for next round MAR sheets checked and secure

Having completed the housekeeping, everything is secure and complete, report to the most senior person on duty any issues arising from the round, including:

Errors refusals, observation concerns stock issues

Refusal

You will experience refusal to take medication and it is a person's right to do that, always remember this. Politely, ask "why" because that might be the opening for them to change their mind. Do not be tempted to be pushy, refused is refused; tell them that you will come back at the end of the round to see if they have changed their mind. Record this on the MAR as you learned earlier in this training programme (red R etc) At the end of the round, they may have changed their mind, if they have administered and record this, if not, informs the most senior person on duty who will take charge of the situation. Either way, the most senior person on duty must be informed.

Dining Room Medication Rounds

Studies have shown medication administration in dining rooms and busy communal areas are common cause of errors, it should not happen.

Tempting, everyone congregated together gets it done more quickly!

Not only are there issues of privacy and dignity etc. what studies have shown is that such environments for medicating are hotspots for mistakes: Increased interruptions greater distractions less easy to pay attention

Client's mind elsewhere too much going on unlocked carts creating security lapses poor infection control paperwork mistakes

Paperwork delays

Obviously, a possible exception to this is a specific "with food" medication, but, remember such meds are usually before or after food which still means it can be done more privately and quietly with less risk of error.

Doctors and MAR Sheets

Doctors are not formally required to sign MAR sheets or care plan entries although a good working relationship with an understanding doctor gains such entries.

Although pressed for time, doctors know the importance of the MAR and will readily annotate where they feel it is appropriate and helpful. Furthermore, they know this helps them maintain the more overall medication picture of that client – everybody benefits.

Whenever a doctor, medical practitioner etc. visits a client the MAR should always be available for them because it contributes to their understanding of what is going on, including the involvement of non-prescription medications.

Eating and Drinking

Some medications have “do” and others “do not” instructions regarding food, drink, alcohol etc. This must be recorded on the MAR and you must check it. Observe – if someone is not complying with their drug/eating/drinking regime, inform the most senior person on duty who will take charge of the matter. Record having passed on the concern in the MAR.

Liquid Medication

Liquid medication must always be dispensed form the container, bottle into the clean medication cap at eye level to make absolutely sure the measure is correct

If you are preparing a crushed medication in a liquid solution, the same applies – prepared at eye level. This also ensures the solution is properly absorbed because you can see it is.

Crushing Medication

Crushing medication changes the way it will be absorbed by the body this could reduce its benefit to the client or harm them, it is not an ideal option.

It is possible, maybe due to a swallowing problem, for example, crushing is necessary – that is not your decision, nor is it your manager's decision. That decision belongs to the prescriber, usually the doctor, who may choose an alternative drug whose properties are less affected by crushing.

Always ask, "is there a suitable alternative, liquid medication perhaps? Because there may well be.

Record the final choice and its reason why, on the care plan and MAR together with the pharmacists instructions on the crushing process etc. Check with the pharmacist the suitability of mixing the crushed pill/s with water, juice etc. to make it easier to administer. If the manufacturer says not to crush, check carefully with the pharmacist.

The pill crusher must be a properly purchased pill crusher for that purpose, not some design of your own, and it must be kept clean and free of cross contamination if more than one client's medication is to be crushed as well.

Both the medication store and med. Cart there must be an alphabetical list of "do not crush" medications clearly on display to prevent mistakes.

Note:

Crushing is not the same as convert medication, we are not secretly hiding the medication in a deceptive manner, and we are making it easier for a consenting client to take their medication more easily to benefit from its purpose.

Convert Medication

Convert medication is the intentional administration of medication without the client's knowledge, therefore, without their consent and in a deceptive manner – they have no idea they have been drugged.

Ask yourself, if something went wrong, would a judge say we had acted in the client's best interests or would the judge say we had acted deceitfully and abused the client's rights? Your answer to this is a useful test to what you re or is proposing to do!

It would clearly be totally unacceptable to give someone drugs without their knowledge or consent if they were able to make informed decisions on the matter and would be an infringement of their rights. If they had refused, then "no" is "no" and that is that. Convert medication in this situation would be completely wrong.

Incapability to offer informed consent:

This, possibly, is a different matter because the person may be unable to make an informed decision within their interests or otherwise. Again, this is not a matter of choice for you or your manager; it belongs to the healthcare team, friends, relatives, doctor etc. Any authority to medicate covertly must be in writing from the client's representative/s and/or doctor who will advise on the method of medication.

That written authority will be kept in the client's confidential file. Furthermore, we will notify our inspectorate that we are medicating covertly and have been authorised to do so. Under no other circumstances is convert medication acceptable. Unless the person has been detained in hospital under a treatment section of the Mental Health Act 1983.

Emergency situations:

Unless we have written instruction to the contrary, in the case of a genuine emergency we may partake in concert medication on the written authority of a medical practitioner.

Missing a Dose

In most situations, missing one dose is not a problem; it might allow a slight flare up of the problems.

In a care home, there is no legitimate excuse for accidentally missing a dose at all. Self-medicating people, those living at home present more of a problem.

Always record a missed dose on the MAR and care plan and notify the most senior person on duty who will take the necessary action. Check, what does the manufacturer say about catching back up on that dose and how does it affect the frequency of the next dose after that one, ask the pharmacist.

Regularly missed doses are a different matter and the doctor needs to be informed at the first time of identifying the problem in order to manager it.

Exceeding a Dose

Usually, one exceeded dose may not be a serious problem, but it should, for the sake of safety, be checked with the pharmacist.

In a care home, there is no legitimate excuse for this happening. People who are self-medicating, living at home are more vulnerable.

Intentionally taking an extra dose to get a quicker result is wrong, drugs do not work like that. Always record the taking of an extra dose on the MAR and care plan.

Forgetfulness can be a problem, maybe the person forgot they had already taken a dose earlier. This can become cause for concern and the doctor should be involved. The person may not have overdosed in the sense of taking handfuls of pills at one time but a gradual increase of too many doses too frequently could build up a severe adverse reaction over a few days.

In the case of what one more traditionally thinks of an overdose, our accident procedures apply.

Disposal and Consent

Remember, the medication belongs to the client; it does not belong to us so disposal is not something we can do without their consent. Disposal could arise due to:

- Change of medication • medication has passed its expiry date • It has been refused • it has been chipped, damaged, gone sticky • It has become discoloured, thickened • the person has died (seven days allowing) • it has been discontinued
- it has been withdrawn • The client going to live elsewhere, taking it with them

Firstly, gaining consent:

- Explain to the client why we have to dispose of it • are they fully informed, can they make informed consent • if they can and consent is given dispose

If informed consent is denied:

- Record this in the care plan and MAR •
  notify the most senior person on duty who will have to manage the issue • the medication must be kept and labelled: - do not use, for disposal, explaining why, dated, initialled and stored separately from "in use" medication but just as securely.

Disposal

We have a disposal record that maintains relevant information regarding the medication and its reason/s for disposal. The disposal record is sequentially numbered, and the relevant number of the record is written on the medication to be disposed. This allows accountability and control of managed drug disposal.

Paying attention to expiry dates is crucial. For example, creams are easy to forget to check, drops may have several years before expiry until open when that may change to only 30 days after opening before they expire.

Disposal is never, under any circumstances:

In the regular waste in the clinical waste down the toilet

Throwing away seemingly harmless refused rill down the toilet seems innocent, but, there could be consequences and we need to have strict return controls when handling medication which is why never down the toilet. S single pill for disposal should be put in a seal top small clear plastic bag (like a tiny freezer bag) and properly labelled.

Disposal must always be back to the pharmacist accompanied by a summary of what is being returned, dose, strength, client, quantity etc.

NON-ORAL ADMINISTRATION

1. Specialised Techniques
2. Gas and Oxygen Safety
3. Eye Medication (Drops)
4. Ear Medication
5. Nasal Drops
6. Inserting an Inhaler
7. Vital Signs
8. Breathing Assessment
9. Measuring Blood Pressure

10. Taking a Pulse

Specialised Techniques

Most medications are taken by mouth (orally) either as tablets, capsules, liquids, etc. Sometimes, these are not appropriate or effective enough and alternative more specialised techniques need to be used. For example: ▪ sub-cutaneous injection ▪ blood sugar testing ▪ rectal ▪ vaginal ▪ gas, oxygen ▪ percutaneous endoscope gastrostomy (PEG) – feeding tube.

Important note

This training resource does not explain these techniques. You are not to conduct or even attempt to conduct these techniques above unless a) trained by a suitably qualified medical practitioner who has b) confirmed in writing that you have c) demonstrated competence to do so under their supervision.

If anyone ever asks you to do any of the above and you have not been properly trained with written confirmation of competence you are not to do any of the above, no matter who asks you to!

Gas and Oxygen Safety

Even though you may not have been trained to administer gas, which is usually oxygen, the fact that oxygen may be in use where you are working means you have to work in a manner that respects gas, oxygen safety.

Oxygen is a key component of fire and is highly flammable. Added to which, pressurised oxygen tanks are explosive, they are dangerous, and have to be treated with respect. You must not use oxygen, no matter who asks you to, unless: ▪ properly trained ▪ authorised as competent, in writing.

Risk Assessment

Where gases, like oxygen, are stored and/or in use means there must be risk assessments and the presence of them reflected specifically in your fire risk assessments as well.

Signs

Any room with oxygen, or other gas, in – whether in use or not – must have an appropriate and visible sign stating: ▪ compressed gas – oxygen (etc.) ▪ no smoking ▪ no naked flames

Regulators

Never tamper or fiddle with a regulator on any gas bottle or cylinder unless specifically trained by a competent person, again, which should be supported by written confirmation of your competence.

The supplier of the oxygen, usually the pharmacist, is responsible for its service and safe condition – subject to our storage and handling responsibilities, etc.

Emergencies:

If we have an emergency – particularly a fire – the emergency service must be told immediately that we have pressurised

gas/oxygen on site – where it is, how much of it there is, etc.

Storage

Dry and clean no extremes of heat/cold ▪ under cover and away from flammable sources, smoking, bonfires, etc. suitable warning notices must be displayed full cylinders must be stores separately from empty ones the pharmacist will advise on whether stored lying down or standing up security – they must be unable to be stolen.

Leaks

A "hissing" sound will suggest there is a leak and you must act immediately: notify the pharmacist turn off the supply remove the cylinder to a safe place never try to repair or patch up a leak.

Using cylinders

Take care – do not drop, bump, knock them, etc. they must only be moved using an appropriate trolley for that purpose ▪ they must be secured to the trolley when being moved ▪ empty cylinders must be notified for collection immediately.

Eye Medication (Drops)

Infection control procedures apply Wear suitable protective equipment, especially gloves Ensure absolute privacy and dignity for the client check – is that the right drop for that person? Check – both eyes or just one, which one? Remove cap – follow standard medication procedures The person sits upright Tilt the head slightly back, make sure they are comfortable Using your thumb and forefinger, gently separate the eyelids Form a small pocket at the lower eyelid between eye and eyelid to catch the drop Gently drop the prescribed drop into the eye, following the manufacturer's instructions, catching it is the pocket mentioned above Make sure you do not touch any part of the eye with the drop container The person blinks gently so you can wipe away any excess drop(s) with paper tissue If more than one drop has to be applied, follow the above sequence, one drop at a time ▪ Replace the cap on the drop container ▪ They open their eyes ▪ If, at any time, the client is uncomfortable, stop before starting again.

Ear Medication

Infection control procedures apply ▪ Wear suitable protective equipment, especially gloves ▪ Ensure absolute privacy and dignity for the client ▪ Proper medication administration practices apply ▪ Check – is this the right drop for that person? ▪ Check – both ears or one ear, which one? ▪ The person turns their head so the ear to be cared for faces upwards ▪ Put the ear medication into warm water; it has to be body temperature ▪ Clean the outer area of the area with cotton swabs – do not put them inside the ear canal Remove cap from the drop container ▪ Hold the ear lobe and gently move it so as to improve access to the ear canal ▪ Apply the prescribed dose of ear drop to the ear canal ▪ Replace cap to the drop container Using a small ball of cotton wool, block the ear canal so the medication cannot escape ▪ Following the manufacturer's instructions; the client holds their head with their ear facing upwards for as long as prescribed Remove the cotton wool ball, into clinical waste.

Nasal drops

Infection control procedures apply ▪ Wear suitable protective equipment, especially gloves ▪ Ensure absolute privacy and dignity for the client ▪ Proper medication administration practices apply ▪ Check – are these the drops for that client? ▪ Check – both nostrils or one nostril, which ones? ▪ Ensure the client is sitting comfortably

They blow their nose to clear the nasal area ▪ The person tilts their head back ▪Remove th4e cap from the drop container ▪ Apply the nose drops in accordance with prescription and manufacturer's instructions – number of drops, frequency ▪ They breathe through their mouth, keeping their head back for a couple of minutes, as instructed by the prescription ▪ With paper towel in front of their nose, they bring their head forwards; the paper towel catches any excess medication ▪ Clean their nose/face ▪ Make sure they are comfortable and advise them not to blow their nose for some while, thereby allowing the medication to be effective ▪ If at any time they are unhappy, stop, before carrying on appropriately.

Inserting an Inhaler

▪Infection control procedures apply ▪ Wear suitable protective equipment, especially gloves ▪ Proper medication administration practices apply ▪ Check – is that inhaler prescribed for use by that person? ▪ Remove cap from the inhaler and shake the inhaler well ▪ Have the client breathe out ▪ Immediately, they put the inhaler mouthpiece into their mouth and make a firm seal around the mouthpiece with their lips ▪ Whilst pressing the inhaler, they breathe in deeply ▪ they must hold their breath for at least 1-seconds (see manufacturer's instructions) ▪ Clean the mouthpiece before replacing the cap ▪ Ensure the client is comfortable.

Vital Signs

Some medications may involve the checking of certain vital signs: ▪ Blood pressure ▪ Breathing ▪ Pulse ▪ Temperature.

It is essential that such checks are properly recorded on the correct chart at the time of medication and vital signs' checking in the same way that the MAR is recorded immediately.

Breathing Assessment

Average breathing for an adult is 12 to 20 breaths per minute ▪ Follow infection control procedures ▪ Wear appropriate protective equipment ▪ Make sure the client is comfortable ▪ Are there any specific breathing difficulties? ▪ Is there any noise when breathing, such as wheezing, etc? ▪ Does their breathing cause them to cough? ▪ Watch the chest; how many breaths per minute? (You will need a timer) ▪ How even is the rhythm of their breathing? ▪ How deep or shallow is their breathing? ▪ What does their colour tell you; for example, blue around the lips, etc? ▪ Is their breathing symmetric? ▪ Does breathing cause them pain – where, when, etc? ▪ A good practice is to count their breaths by pretending to take their pulse – the client doesn't concentrate on their breathing!

Measuring Blood Pressure

Follow infection control procedures ▪ Wear appropriate protective equipment ▪ Make sure the room is warm ▪ Position the person so they can rest their arm flat, ideally about the same height as their heart ▪ Expose the arm between the elbow and shoulder ▪ Wrap the cuff around the exposed area of the arm, the lower part of the cuff should be about 2 cm above the inside of the elbow ▪ Inflate the cuff, follow the manufacturer's instructions as some sphygmomanometers require the measurement of the pulse whilst doing this ▪ The instructions will tell you when to stop inflation and slowly deflate the cuff ▪ The first measurement is the diastolic pressure ▪ The instruction for your sphygmomanometers will tell you how to identify these measurements ▪ Record these measurements now – do not wait until later Completely deflate the cuff and remove it ▪ Is the client comfortable?

Taking a Pulse

Do not use your thumb ▪ Use your index and middle fingers together ▪ Use the "pads" of your fingers Find the pulse on the underneath of the person's wrist Find the pulse on the person's neck (to the side of their windpipe) ▪ It should beat about once every second.

Practice finding a pulse on some of your colleagues!

Controlled Drugs

Controlled drugs (often abbreviated to CD) are those drugs and medications that:

have the likelihood of being extremely harmful ▪ have no recognised medical use ▪ and /or drugs that are not generally in the public interest

Possession of them without a prescription is illegal. Therefore, their presence has to be strictly controlled, there is no room for error – but why should that be different from any other drugs we administer?

The legal implications of having such drugs present are important, in some cases; their presence may even be licensed.

There are many controlled drugs, you may have heard of some of them, for example:

Cocaine ▪ Morphine ▪ Opium and related drugs ▪ Amphetamines ▪ Barbiturates ▪ Anabolic steroids ▪ Benzodiazepines ▪ Major (and some minor) stimulants

Authorisation to Administer

As you know, we keep a published list of those persons authorised to administer non-controlled drugs. Being on that list has not authorised you to become involved in any part in the administration of controlled drugs.

There is an additional list which is known as our Controlled Drug Authorisation Register

To have been put on this authorisation list means we have been convinced that you are competent to administer such medication based upon training, supervision, observation etc. To remain on that list you will be supervised annually to ensure you have retained that competence.

If you are not on that register (list) you are not – under any circumstance at all – to have contact in any way with controlled drug whilst conducting your duties or associated activities. To do so could result in disciplinary action, which, according to the circumstances, could lead to dismissal for gross misconduct.

Handling Illegal Drugs

Being in possession of drugs not prescribed to you, especially if they are controlled drugs is illegal. Keeping them, or allowing them to be kept, for a client could result in you having committed a criminal offence for which you could lose your livelihood, even

Controlled Drugs (CD) Disposal

Once more, the disposal process should not be dissimilar with good practice in the disposal of non-controlled drugs just that bit more rigorous in place.

There is no accepted alternative to the disposal of controlled drugs – always to the pharmacist.

The CD Register will be double signed and dated, as with all CD transactions, and a Controlled Drugs Return Form completed to be given to the pharmacist (or their representative) for signature. This provides evidence they have receipt of the medication and not us. This is filed and kept for at least two years before disposal.

Self-Medication

When a client is self-medicating, a simple “lockable storage” that they would use for non-controlled medication becomes unacceptable.

Whilst the storage is still kept in the client’s room, whilst it is still lockable, it must also be nom-portable – it has to be fixed. Also, where someone is living in a care home, rather than in home care settings, there needs to be a greater reassurance that the CD will not be accidentally or deliberately taken by persons other than to whom it was prescribed.

ERROR MANAGEMENT

- Identifying Errors
- Error Prevention
- Supervision
- Auditing

Identifying Errors

Virtually every medication administration error is a human error – someone got it wrong. The number of errors in medication administration is huge, usually there is no serious consequence, but those errors can and have killed.

On the basis most medications are administered accurately, and the paperwork is completed accurately proves it can be done accurately.

Some important principles

DO NOT RUSH ▪ TAKE CARE ▪ THINK ▪ CHECK.

Several studies in Europe and America over many years show "at best" an 8% medication error rate, rising to between 12% and 15% in some cases. Would you fly with an airline where their error rate was that high? That is a one in ten chance of being given the wrong medication!

How would you feel about your mum, dad, brother, daughter being exposed to that level of mediation risk? Should you expose someone else's loved one to that risk?

How dangerous do you think it could be for some of the people you care for to be given the wrong medication?

What is a medication error?

Basically, anything not specified as the correct use the application of a medication is a medication error. It could result from: ▪ not following manufacturer's instructions ▪ not following the prescriber's/pharmacist's instructions ▪ not following professional standards ▪ not following statutory requirements ▪ poor training ▪ inadequate supervision.

Alternatively, good medication is about

Giving the right medication ▪ At the right time ▪ In the right way ▪ Recording it properly ▪ Identifying problems ▪ Reporting issues ▪ preventing error.

Under the carpet

Never sweep a medication error under the carpet – own up to it NOW. Not doing so could have worse consequences when it is found out, for everyone.

If you tell the most senior person on duty *immediately*, we can do something about it. You will not be disciplined for being responsible enough to deal with the error fast – sweep it under the carpet and that is a different matter.

We will always investigate medication error, not to embarrass or punish you, but to learn what went wrong and avoid it happening again – why not try to gain some good from a bad situation.

When you report the error

Having informed the most senior person on duty immediately the error occurred: ▪ Stop the med. round We will assume the worst, better safe than sorry ▪ The most senior person on duty will take charge of the situation ▪ the pharmacist will be contacted for advice If necessary, the doctor will be called ▪ The person who made the error will complete a Medication Error Report.

After the immediate situation has settled down: ▪ The manager will review the Medication Error Report ▪ Action will be implemented to prevent recurrence.

Error Prevention

Wrong person

Amazingly, this is a very common error – giving the wrong medication to the wrong person.

To prevent this: ▪ Is the person clearly described on the MAR? ▪ Is there a recent picture of the person on the MAR? ▪ Did you check - is this MAR for that person? ▪ Did you check - is this the right medication for this person?

Use by dates

Medication exceeding its “use by” date must be disposed of, yet, many surveys find this not happening!

Plan ahead, have we got enough supply to prevent the risk of this happening? Check – before you administer: is this in date?

Dose changes

Never change a dose, this is not your responsibility. The only person that can do that is someone suitable qualified to do so; the doctor, for example.

Check – before you administer; has a dose change been authorised?

With or without food or fluid

The presence of too little or too much food or fluid when medicating can alter the effect of the medication which can harm the client. For example, NSAIDs must be taken with or immediately after food. Not doing so could cause stomach bleeding.

Check – What are the instructions regarding food and fluid and the medication you are about to administer?

Inadequate shaking

Several liquid medications require shaking to get the ingredients evenly distributed. If not, you give the client too much of one and not enough of another, which imbalances their medication and could cause them harm.

Check – if it needs shaking/is the top on properly?/shake it well

Decanting

Never decant medication from one container to another. If a new supply is received, never top it up with an existing or old supply.

Putting tablets into a compliance aid is decanting; this is not your job – don't do it!

Supervision

Regular supervision is an essential part of good management and has a significant role to play in safe medication administration.

To uphold your competence and refresh your confidence in keeping you as an authorised person, we will conduct one supervision per year, focused upon the practical element of medication administration.

Auditing

Every well-managed business audit its performance; how it is actually doing compared with how it should be doing.

An annual medication audit is an essential part of a good medication management system, and part of good quality management.

Involving your pharmacist in your annual medication audit can be a good idea; they have a "fresh set of eyes" to see things differently whilst appreciating what you are doing and why.

Self-audit is perfectly legitimate; you simply need an audit tool to work with to ensure the audit is robust, worthwhile and makes you look where you might not want to! This also means you are most likely to put right error and, or prevent, others arising.

The audit findings should form part of your overall quality management audit and the findings should be kept for seven years.

Chapter 3 Approx. Page 198-223

INFECTION CONTROL

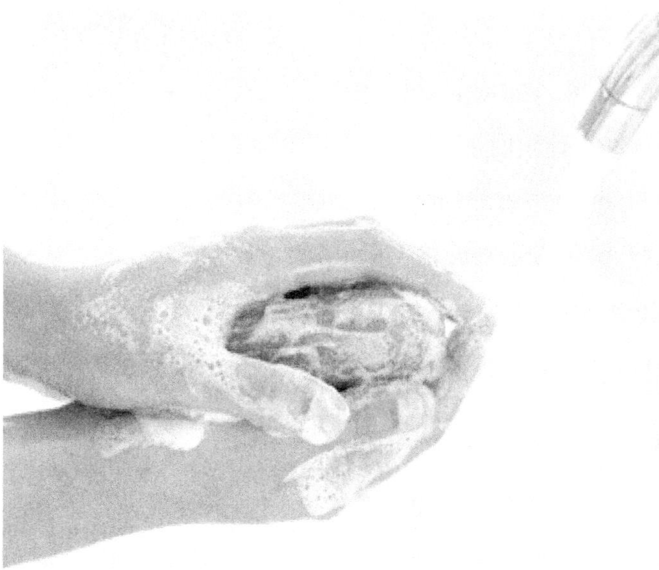

Legislation

Introduction

This booklet is to give a summary of infection and how to prevent infection in a care environment.

As new types emerge ▪ Resistance to antibiotics is increasing ▪ Service Users are becoming more dependant, less mobile etc ▪ Old infections are re-emerging ▪ Increased use of invasive procedures ▪ Some new medicines reduce immunity ▪ Staff pressure ▪ Poor understanding of good hygiene

At Risk Groups

The elderly ▪ The infirm ▪ Those who are ill ▪ Those with weakened immunity ▪ Those who are convalescing ▪ ▪Pregnant mothers ▪ The very young

Legislation

Health and Safety at Work Act (safe practices) ▪ Environmental Protection Act (waste) ▪ Personal Protective Equipment or PPE (protective equipment) ▪ COSHH (substances including chemicals, micro-

organisms etc) ▪ RIDDOR (reporting incidents, accidents, diseases etc) ▪
Public Health Regulations (public health) ▪ Provision of Work Equipment or PUWER (equipment safety) ▪ Medical Devices (medical equipment safety) ▪ Disposal of Healthcare Waste (waste disposal) ▪ Management Regulations (including risk assessment) Employer's Responsibilities Assessing the risks ▪ Providing and maintaining safe equipment and ways of working ▪Maintaining a safe workplace with safe entrance and exit ▪ Providing adequate welfare facilities ▪ Providing information, instruction, training and
supervision ▪ Consulting staff to gain their co-operation and commitment

Employee's Responsibilities

Taking responsibility for your own safety ▪ Taking care not to harm others by what you do or by what you don't do ▪ Co-operating with your employer ▪ Not interfering with anything provided in the interests of safety, health or welfare ▪ Informing the person in charge of dangers, even if they're not immediate ▪ To work as trained

The Law in Practice

Identifying the problems (risk assessment) ▪ Relevant policies, procedures and practices ▪ Induction, training and appraisal ▪ Monitoring, reviewing and making appropriate changes

Reporting of Injuries and Diseases

By law, we must report certain injuries, diseases and dangerous occurrences – this training materials focuses on the disease element of that.

Where a member of staff or volunteer is off work for three consecutive days or more (including days off and weekends) due to work related injury or ill health we report this to the HSE. Any disease, such as communicable diseases, must be notified to the HSE.

Substances Hazardous to Health

Always read and follow the instructions on the tin, container etc

Always wear suitable gloves, apron etc when necessary ▪ Do not leave chemicals, etc lying about ▪ Put things away properly as soon as you finish using them ▪ Do not decant items unless absolutely necessary ▪ If you do decant always clearly mark the new container with what is in it

Understanding the Problem

Micro-organisms

Viruses ▪ Fungi ▪ Bacteria

How do micro-organisms become a problem?

They access human skin, tissue etc ▪ Then they get into the blood stream ▪ Here they multiply or incubate (sometime days, sometimes months) ▪ Body cells, body tissue etc become injured ▪ The host becomes ill

Two key words:

Virulence – how able the micro-organism is to invade you

Toxicity – how able the micro-organism is to damage human tissue

Parasites

Lice ▪ Fleas ▪ Scabies

Lice

Small blood sucking insects ▪ Transmitted by close physical contact ▪ Cause itching

Fleas

May bite you if cat or dog etc not available ▪ Can survive for months outside a host, waiting ▪ Require thorough insecticide distribution to eliminate them

Scabies

Tiny skin burrowing mite ▪ Generally, requires reasonable skin-to-skin contact to transmit ▪ But, some (Norwegian scabies) are highly contagious.

Fungi

Athlete's foot ▪ Thrush

Viruses

HIV ▪ Rabies ▪ Herpes

To kill a virus:

Excessive heat is require over time, boiling ▪ Removal from living cells

Bacteria

Broadly, there are three categories of bacteria:

Beneficial ▪ Spoilage ▪ Pathogenic

Beneficial bacteria

Create medicines ▪ Digest food ▪ Treat sewage

Spoilage Bacteria

Make things rot, go mouldy ▪ Cause smells

Pathogenic Bacteria

Cause poisoning ▪ Cause disease

Pathogenic Bacteria

People ▪ Pests ▪ Pets ▪ Foods ▪ Air ▪ Dirt ▪ Water … everywhere!

Bacteria – Ideal Conditions

Food ▪ Warmth ▪ Moisture ▪ Time

Bacteria – Ideal conditions

Food - The protein that we need in our diet happens to be just what bacteria like

Warmth - Our body temperature is 37°C which happens to be the favourite temperature for bacteria as well - Below 5°C bacteria "go to sleep", they become dormant and over 63oC many begin to die, although not all

Bacteria – Ideal conditions

Moisture - Just like us, bacteria need to drink – they need moisture

Time - The more time we have available, the more we can do and so it is for bacteria as well. The more time they are left alone, the more they can multiply, infect and make you ill.

To Stop Bacteria Multiplying

Make it too hot for them – boil them and kill them ▪ Don't let them drink – dehydrate them by removing the moisture ▪ Harass them – don't give them any time to multiply

Chain of Infection

Means of Transmission

Direct ▪ Indirect ▪ Droplet ▪ Airborne ▪ Faecal-oral

Means of Transmission

Direct - Skin to skin - Skin to object or object to skin

Indirect - Skin to object to skin - Animal to object to skin - - Indirect is via a physical intermediary, it is not direct

Means of Transmission

Droplet - Micro-organisms travel to host from source quickly at close range through droplets passed in the air from source to host - Talking, coughing, sneezing, etc

Airborne - Micro-organisms travel for hours, often some distance away through droplets in the air

Means of Transmission

Faecal-oral - A cycle is created whereby micro-organisms travel faeces and end up being swallowed by the host – contaminated water, food etc - Often results in stomach upsets, diarrhoea, vomiting etc

Commonly Touched Surfaces

Taps ▪ Toilet seats ▪ Toilet door handles ▪ Bars of soap

Telephones ▪ Handling equipment ▪ Furniture ▪ Cooking utensils ▪ Beds ▪ Mattresses

Hand washing ▪ Clean environment Decontaminating equipment ▪ Personal protective equipment (PPE) Laundry management ▪ Waste management Managing contact with blood, body fluids etc Handling sharps, dealing with needlestick Handling specimens Possible isolation of a Service User.

Risk Assessment

All the possible infections you might encounter ▪ Who or what are the sources? ▪ What are the means of transmission? ▪ Who or what are the possible hosts? What is the likelihood of the spread of infection ▪ If infection spreads, what could the consequences by? What action are you going to take to target the potential problem? ▪ Who will take that action and when? ▪ How will you know it has been done?

Hand Washing

Not accepting excuses for not doing it ▪ Making time to do it ▪ Getting into the habit of doing it ▪ Nag colleagues to do it ▪ Enough ... Sinks? - Paper towels? - Soap dispensers? - Hand scrubs? - Nail brushes - ... etc ▪ Fit lever operated mixer taps to hand wash basins ▪ Owners and managers – lead by example

Wash Hands When ...

before contact with a Service User ▪ After contact with a Service User ▪ After touching your hair, face etc Having used the toilet ▪ Having handled laundry, bedmaking ▪ Before handling food ▪ During handling food ▪ After handling food ▪ Before and after eating Before and after feeding a Service User ▪ Before and after smoking ▪ After handling pets ▪ After handling waste – general or clinical

You have been cleaning ▪ Before and after medicating Before and after working with dressings, etc Before and after toileting, bathing etc, a Service

User ▪ Before you put on protective gloves ▪ After you took them off in case the removal contaminated your hands

Types of Hand Decontamination

Routine ▪ Antiseptic hand rub

Types of Hand Decontamination

Routine - Removes transient micro-organisms - Using soap and water, the friction and "sticking to" effect of the soap "rubs off" the micro-organisms - Dry your hands properly - You might then use a hand rub as well afterwards

Types of Hand Decontamination

Antiseptic hand rub - Use the same techniques as for handwashing - Follow the manufacturer's instructions - The hand rub is usually alcohol based - It does not clean the hands, washing does that, but it "adds value" to the cleaning and lengthens the time the hands benefit from the washing

Handwashing Technique

Wet hands ▪ Soap Hands - Use soap dispensers not soap bars

Lather - Work up a lather including wrists

Wash - Rub hands thoroughly including between fingers for about 20 seconds

Rinse - Rinse with clean running warm water - Avoid touching the side of the sink

Dry Dry hands and wrists with disposable paper towels - Do not use towelling towels

Dry Your Hands Properly

Proper hand drying:

Disposable paper towels ▪ Easily accessed via wall mounted dispensers ▪ Throw away into foot-controlled pedal bin – no need to touch the bin with your clean hands!

Skin Care

To prevent damage: - Wet your hands before soaping them

Rinse the soap off thoroughly - Dry them properly – Particularly between fingers

Hand cream: - Applying hand cream regularly reduces the "drying out" effect of such regular hand washing - Do not share the hand cream since that becomes itself a means of transmission spreading micro-organisms

Physical Decontamination

Cleaning ▪ Disinfecting ▪ Sterilising

Environmental Cleanliness

A planned cleaning schedule ▪ Suitable cleaning products Suitable cleaning equipment ▪ Proper induction, training and supervision of cleaning staff ▪ Attentive management

Environmental Cleanliness

Managing clinical and general waste properly ▪ Good housekeeping ▪ Good handwashing facilities ▪ Good ventilation and circulation of fresh air ▪ Easy clean facilities, furnishings etc

Cleaning Schedule

Daily ▪ Weekly ▪ Monthly ▪ Annually

Cleaning

Cleaning products: - Proprietary products - Washing up liquid - Detergents - Hot soapy water

Products are recorded, as appropriate, in our COSHH file

Cleaning

Cleaning equipment - To avoid cross-contamination, cloths are used once and thrown away - Wet, cleaned surfaces are dried with paper towels which are thrown away - Carpet machines are empties and cleaned after use - Where possible, we colour code cleaning equipment to reduce the possibility of cross-contamination

Cleaning

Carpet cleaning - Daily vacuum - Shampoo treated as required - Spillages removed immediately - Urine spillage removed, shampoo treated immediately

Cleaning

Mops and Buckets: - Change water regularly, must stay hot - Store mops upside down - Change mop heads regularly

Bathroom cleaning: - We appreciate that bacteria like the warm, moist bathroom environment - Baths, sinks, etc cleaned with detergent after use - Disinfected after use if Service User has stomach bug

Cleaning

Bed Frames: - Regularly overlooked for cleaning - On a regular cleaning schedule - Hot water and detergent - Dried quickly and thoroughly

Domestic Staff

General cleaning duties ▪ Cleaning schedules ▪ Use of cleaning equipment ▪ Body fluids, blood and relevant spillages etc ▪ Sharps and needlestick situations

Clinical and general waste handling ▪ Linen and laundry

Bed making ▪ Housekeeping

Drying

Scrape off surplus residues, dirt etc ▪ Wash with hot water and detergent ▪ Use clean hot water until detergent washed off ▪ Leave the disinfectant on long enough to kill bacteria ▪ Use clean hot water until disinfectant washed off ▪ Use disposable paper towel to dry off quickly (avoid using cloths for drying)

Disinfecting Using Chemicals

Before disinfecting: - Clean with hot soapy water first

When using disinfectants, DO: - Following manufacturer's instructions via the data sheets - Conduct and retain COSHH assessments (COSHH file) - Dilute, where instructed to do so, accurately - Use Personal Protective Equipment (PPE) - Clean up spillages, immediately - Make sure the user knows what they are doing

Disinfecting Using Chemicals

When using disinfectants, DO NOT: - Mix with other chemicals - Store where they are not secure - Use them unless you have to

Some Useful Disinfectants

Sterilisation

Their servicing ▪ Risk of scalding ▪ Checking seals, valves ▪ Monitoring their effectiveness

Exposure to Blood, Body Fluids

Bleeding ▪ Open wounds, ulcers, sores, etc ▪ Broken skin tissue ▪ Saliva ▪ Urine ▪ Faeces ▪ Vomit ▪Tears Being bitten or scratched by someone ▪ Dressings Catheters ▪

Needlestick injury

Spillages ▪ Blood ▪ Body fluids ▪ Bathing ▪ In the kitchen ▪ Whilst cleaning ▪ Spilt waste ▪ Split bags

Cleaning Up A Spillage

Act immediately ▪ Do not leave it for someone else Wear disposable gloves ▪ Wear a disposable apron Clean up with a paper towel ▪ Disinfect properly Dispose of clinical waste ▪ You might need a sodium hydrochloride solution

Sharps

Safe use of sharps:

Do ▪ Dispose of your own sharps ▪ Keep sharps boxes near where they are required ▪ Keep sharps boxes where persons may not be injured ▪ Treat open razors etc as sharps because they are sharps! Wear gloves/apron if you might come into contact with blood ▪ Take precautions when cleaning up spillages

Sharps

Don't Keep sharps in pockets ▪ Presheath needles Keep sharps boxes near radiators or in direct sunlight ▪ Fill sharps boxes more than 75% full

Safe disposal of sharps: ▪ Don't put sharps into empty cans or bottles etc ▪ Dispose of sharps boxes when 75% full

Seal sharp boxes before disposal ▪ Don't place sharps boxes in plastic bags before disposal ▪ Have sharps boxes professionally collected and disposed of regularly

Needlestick Policy

Allowed the wound to bleed – don't suck ▪ Clean the wound with running water ▪ Cover with a waterproof dressing ▪ Inform the most senior person on duty Complete the accident book ▪ Visit your GP or even A&E in certain circumstances

Needlestick Policy

A sharp item punctures your skin or that of someone else ▪ Someone in our care scratches you or someone else ▪ A person or animal bites you or someone else

Specimens

Service Users full name ▪ Our name, address and telephone number

Personal Protective Equipment

Gloves: - Disposable gloves protect the wearer from skin to skin/surface contact with the person or equipment they are working with to reduce transmission of micro-organisms. - They must be worn once, for one task, and then thrown away into the clinical waste.

Personal Protective Equipment

Wear disposable gloves when exposed to: ▪ Blood Body fluids ▪ Hazardous substances ▪ Broken skin Contaminated surfaces ▪ Contaminated items Handling laundry, linen etc ▪ Cleaning situations the list is huge

Personal Protective Equipment

Gloves are: ▪ Put on before contact with person/item etc.

Used once only ▪ Taken off after contact with person/item etc.

Thrown into clinical waste immediately after use ▪ Not instead of hand washing

Personal Protective Equipment

Latex allergy: ▪ Some people are allergic to latex (NRL) gloves which can show from a mild rash to anaphylaxis(a severe reaction). If using gloves causes skin problems, seek medical advice – don't ignore it.

No gloves is not an option, therefore, to avoid problems use:

Neoprene gloves ▪ Powder free gloves ▪ Vinyl gloves (not in body fluid contact situation)

Disposable aprons: ▪ Use where there may be contact with body fluids ▪ Use once only ▪ Throw into clinical waste when used ▪ Wash hand before throwing away

Masks: Used where there is a genuine risk of body fluids entering the carers mouth, nose. For example, caring for someone with TB would require wearing a mask.

Worn once only, into clinical waste after use, wash hands immediately.

Eye protection: Rarely used in non- hospital situations , protect the eyes from contamination with body fluids.

Barrier Precautions

A service User colonised by certain micro- organisms may need extra emphasis placed upon reducing direct and/or indirect transmission of infection. Examples could include gastric infections, MRSA and precautions might include:

Not sharing a room ▪ Wearing the right PPE Keeping equipment and surfaces scrupulously clean ▪ Not sharing equipment, for example a hoist sling ▪ Clean spillages away immediately

Gastro-intestinal infections: Where the Service User is vomiting, having diarrhoea etc.

Avoid using communal toilets ▪ Disinfect commodes. Pans etc. immediately after use ▪ Keep Service User clean

Ensure their hand hygiene is of the highest standard ▪ Apply the above points

Isolation

The likelihood of a Service User transmitting infection to others could be extremely high requiring isolation. Isolation is under the instruction and guidance of appropriate medical advice

Food hygiene practices compliment infection control practices by specifically controlling the spread of infection throughout any food handling situation.

Personal Hygiene

Since we are both carriers and transmitters of micro-organisms, our personal hygiene is important in order to prevent the spread of infection.

Skin:

Washing everyday reduces the number of micro-organisms on our body that might spread infection. This does not replace regular hand washing.

Hair:

Keep it clean, tidy and tied back – wash your hand after touching your hair.

Mouth, nose, ears:

Wash your hands after touching your face, particularly after blowing your nose.

Jewellery:

Straps, rings etc. harbour bacteria which makes jewellery undesirable in care environments – particularly earrings, piercing etc

Cuts and grazes:

Cover with waterproof dressing to prevent transmission of micro-organisms.

Diarrhoea and vomiting:

Report to the Registered Manager with the problem, you should not come to work if you have diarrhoea and vomiting.

Staff and Visitor Toilet Facilities

Separate provision is made for staff and visitors to use the toilets. Those toilets will always have, as a minimum:

Toilet roll holder ▪ Supply of toilet roll ▪ Wall mounted soap dispenser ▪ Soap in the dispenser ▪ Paper towel dispenser ▪ Paper in the dispenser ▪ Paper waste bin ▪ Secure clothes handling hooks ▪ Mirror Clean nail brush

Always wash your hands after using the toilet.

Uniforms

During a shift, the clothes you wear will probably gather and harbour micro-organisms that could cause infection. Therefore, we supply enough uniform changes so that each day you can wear a new, clean uniform.

The uniform worn today should be laundered tonight on a hot wash and dried as quickly as possible to prevent the growth of micro-organisms.

This also applies to the wearing of your own clothes.

Linen and Laundry

Always wear disposable gloves and disposable apron when working with linen and laundry (whether it is soiled or not) and keep it stored in the designated areas ▪ Wash your hands thoroughly and regularly ▪

Risks related to linen and laundry infection control are recorded in our COSHH file.

Soiled linen: Soiled linen (any linen contaminated with body fluids) goes immediately from the bed or wearer into a red bag (alginate bag) so it is clearly identifiable as soiled. Unsoiled linen goes into the white bags, so it is clearly identifiable as unsoiled.

Soiled laundry must be washed separately in suitable facilities to at least 65°C for at least 10 minutes (71°C for 3 minutes) before going into a standard wash.

Lighting and ventilation

We ensure the laundry is well ventilated either by fresh air and/or extractor units so that there are no fumes , smells, unnecessary humidity and/or heat levels etc. which limits the potential growth of micro-organisms.

Sluicing

Never in the sink ▪ Always in the washing machine on a sluice programme.

Sluicing

Hand sluicing of laundry, pans etc. is strictly forbidden equipment is improved to ensure there are no reason to hand sluice.

Before laundering, soiled items must be suitably sluiced in the correct equipment provided for the correct period of time.

Sluice machine

Discreetly marked ▪ Secure ▪ Such that they do not disturb the Service User

Never wash your hands where soiled and/or sluiced items may have been and never put soiled and/or sluiced items in or near sinks etc. dedicated for hand washing

Clinical Waste

Blood and other body fluids ▪ Surplus or rejected medication ▪ Needles, razor blades and other sharps Human tissue ▪ Faeces, urine ▪ Used incontinence pads, colostomy bags etc ▪ Disposable bedpans, liners, vomit bowls etc ▪ Used sanitary tampons Used condoms ▪ Items contaminated with any of the above examples

Clinical Waste

Any waste that involves human tissue, human waste products, dressings etc. is clinical waste and must be disposed of as such – never in the regular non clinical waste.

When handling clinical waste, always wear disposable gloves and aprons.

Clinical waste is to be put directed into yellow bags which are handled only by their neck. Yellow bags are only to be used for clinical waste.

When a clinical waste bag is 75% full, tie it off securely at the top and put into a clinical waste bin/s outside which are marked yellow and state ''Clinical Waste Only'' .

By law, the clinical waste bin/s outside have to be locked securely away from other people, pests, vermin etc. It is not mixed with the general waste disposal bins.

General Waste

When a sack is 75% full , tied- the top securely, handle it only by the neck and place it in the general waste bin. Be careful nothing can poke through the sack that might injure the person handling it. ▪ Never allow sacks to sit on or lie around the waste bin outside since this can attract rodents and pests ▪ If the outside bins overflow, the Registered Manager will arrange for additional waste bins to contain the surplus waste.

Pets and Pests

Insects, rodents birds, pets etc. can spread infection by direct or indirect transmission, saliva, dropping etc. Putting food and rubbish etc. away properly helps significantly.

Bites, stings, scratches, etc. could be warning signs, look out for and report them to the registered Manager.

Communicable Diseases

Chicken pox ▪ Cholera ▪ Dysentery ▪ Food poisoning ▪ Hepatitis ▪ Legionnaire disease ▪ Leptospirosis ▪ Malaria ▪ Measles ▪ Meningitis ▪ Mumps ▪ Salmonella ▪ Scarlet fever ▪ Shingles ▪ Smallpox ▪ Tuberculosis ▪ Typhoid ▪ Whooping Cough ▪ Yellow fever

Chapter 4 Approx. pages 224-259

FOOD HYGIENE

FOOD HYGIENE

Food Hygiene

Food Hygiene brings the best current practices and thinking in food hygiene into one simple training package. It is designed to be used by the care provider themselves to instruct any staff member who may be a food handler in food hygiene matters encountered in care provision.

There are four modules which take about 30 to 40 minutes to complete and we recommend a module is taken each week for four weeks. This builds much better understanding by consolidating on learning that has had time to sink in and be put to practice rather than cramming it all into one day with no practical application.

The Law- What it Requires

There are three main pieces of applicable legislation: 1990 Food Safety Act ▪ 1995 Food Safety Regulations 1995 Food Temperature Regulations

What do these pieces of legislation say? ▪ You must provide food and drink that is safe and wholesome Every aspect of food handling must be hygienic, and risks managed ▪ Keep food below 5 C or above 63 C.

The Law- Legal Duties

Legal duties of the owner and/or Registered Manager: Food handling must be hygienic ▪

Premises and equipment must be hygienic ■ Food hazards must be identified and managed ■ Food handlers must be suitably instructed.

Legal duties of the food handler: ■ To work hygienically ■ To follow laid down policy and procedures ■ To wear appropriate clothing ■ To report illness immediately

The Law- Enforcement

Food hygiene is enforced by Environmental Health Officers who have stringent power which include: The right to enter premises with or without your permission The right to take samples, check records etc ■ The right to make you put in place improvements The right to prohibit unhygienic practices.

Penalties: Magistrates Courts can impose: ■£20,000 fines per offence ■ Imprisonment for up to 6 months. Crown Courts can impose: ■ £ unlimited fines ■ imprisonment for up to 2 years. Such action could have huge implication for registered persons and de-registration could arise.

Food Hygiene Policy

It is important to have a clear policy that sets out the intent we have towards good food hygiene. Our food Hygiene Policy states:

Good food hygiene is essential to prevent the risk of food poisoning and the possible transmission of infection. It is always our intention to ensure we provide those in our care with safe, healthy and nutritious food. This applies equally to staff and visitors who also eat food prepared on our premises.

For this reason, any person who is involved in handling food in any way will receive suitable instruction in food hygiene whether that instruction is internally or externally. Such a person will have passed a simple test to ensure they understand good food hygiene before they are allowed to handle food.

This means persons handling food understand food hygiene practices and are personally responsible for any breaches which could lead to disciplinary action, such is the significance we place on good consistent food standards

(Signed by the Registered Manager)

The Significance of Food Hygiene

Poor food hygiene can cause : ■ food poisoning ■ poor reputation ■ complaints ■waste ■ poor morale ■ staff absence ■ loss of income ■ damaged profits ■

fines (non-insurable) ■ imprisonment ■ compensation claims ■ closure ■ lost jobs

Good food hygiene can lead to: ■ legal compliance improved likelihood of more clients ■ retention of clients ■ retention of staff ■ good reputation ■ better income ■ better profitability ■ better job security

The Problem- Food Poisoning : ■ Every day, 300 new cases of food poisoning are reported in the UK Everyday, another 4,000 cases in the UK are estimated as unreported.

Food Poisoning can cause you to suffer: ■ Nausea vomiting ■ abdominal pain ■ diarrhoea ■ fever headache.

Food poisoning can be life threatening, especially to the elderly and/or infirm.

Food Poisoning- At Risk Groups

Anyone can get food poisoning, but certain groups of people are more at risk than others, these “at risk” groups include: ■ Pregnant women ■ The very young Those with weakened immunity ■ Those who are ill ■

Those who are convalescing ■ The elderly ■ The infirm

The Causes of Food Poisoning: ■ The main cause of food poisoning is through eating food contaminated by harmful bacteria ■ It can also be caused by eating food contaminated by harmful substances such as : viruses, chemicals, metals, moulds, poisonous plants, poisonous animals ■ Anything that could contaminate food that might cause a person harm is called a food hazard.

Food Hazards

The three main categories of food hazard are physical, chemical and microbial.

Physical hazards (or contaminants): hair, dust, paint flakes, animal droppings, glass, jewellery, plasters, stones/pips, packaging, insects, bits of equipment. Chemical hazards (or contaminants) ■ cleaning products, chemicals, pesticides, rodent poisons, herbicides, medicines ■ Microbial hazards (or contaminants) ■ bacteria viruses, moulds, tiny parasites. (microbial contaminants are sometimes called microbiological.

Bacteria

Bacteria are the main cause of food contamination, which can lead to food poisoning. However, most bacteria are helpful and only a few are harmful.

The three categories of bacteria are: ■ Beneficial bacteria ■ spoilage bacteria ■ Pathogenic bacteria

Beneficial bacteria assist us to: ■ Create medicines Digest food ■ Treat sewage ■ Produce certain foods

Spoilage bacteria cause food to: ■ Rot ■ Go mouldy Change smell ■ Change colour

Pathogenic bacteria cause : ■ Food poisoning ■ Food diseases.

Pathogenic bacteria, the bacteria that cause food poisoning, come from: ■ People ■ Pests ■ Pets Raw foods ■ Air ■ Dirt

Pathogenic Bacteria- Common Types

Salmonella: ■ Comes from raw meat, poultry, eggs, pets and insects ■ Causes vomiting, diarrhoea and fever within 12 to 36 hours of eating contaminated food

Clostridium: ■ Comes from soil, insects, faeces, dust, raw meat and fish ■ Causes abdominal pain, diarrhoea and breathing difficulties within 12 to 36 hours of eating contaminated food.

E-Coli: ■Comes from gut, sewage, raw meat and water

Causes abdominal pain, diarrhoea, vomiting, fever and even kidney failure within 12 to 24 hours

Listeria: ■ Comes from soft cheeses, salad vegetables and pate ■Causes flu like symptoms within days of eating contaminated food

Staphylococcus Aureus: ■ Comes from the nose, mouth, cuts, boils and raw milk (MRSA is multi resistant form familiar to care providers) ■ Causes abdominal pain, vomiting within 1-6 hours

Bacteria- Ideal Conditions

Bacteria multiply extremely fast when the conditions are right for them. To multiply, they need the right : Food, Warmth, Moisture, Time

Binary Fission:

Bacteria multiply by splitting into two, this is called binary fission.

It takes 10 to 20 minutes for each one to split into two. One bacterium becomes two, those two become four, then eight, sixteen, thirty-two, sixty-four and so on. Within a few hours there can be millions of them.

Food:

The protein that we need in our diet is exactly the same that the bacteria need too. Food rich in protein are very nourishing to bacteria who can thrive in such foods, which is why they are termed as “high risk foods”.

Examples include dairy products, eggs, cooked meats- anything that is rich in protein.

Warmth:

37□C is human body temperature; it also happens to be the temperature in which bacteria thrive. However, bacteria can multiply at temperatures as low as 5□C, and as high as 63□C.

Therefore, 5□C to 63□C is known as the “Danger Zone”.

Below 5□C, bacteria “go to sleep”, they are not dead, only dormant. Above 63□C, bacteria begin to die.

Time:

Like us, the more time we have available the more we can do. The longer time bacteria have to multiply, the more likely they can cause illness and the more serious that illness can be.

How Do Bacteria spread?

Pathogenic bacteria cannot be seen, heard or smelt which makes them invisible to us and, therefore, difficult to know if they are being spread.

That is why anyone handling food must be cautious at all times because you do not know what you are spreading.

There are three types of contamination: □ Direct □Indirect □Cross –contamination

Direct contamination: Where one food directly touches another food.

Indirect contamination: For example, juice dripping from one food to another food.

Cross-contamination: Hands or utensils carrying bacteria from one food to another food.

Stopping Bacteria From Multiplying

There are three main ways bacteria can be prevented from multiplying when handling food in care settings: □Drying □Cooling □Heating

Drying: Removing the moisture that bacteria need to multiply makes them dormant, it doesn't kill them

Keep dried foods and those prone to absorbing moisture in sealed containers and off the floor to prevent them becoming moist or damp.

Cooling: Keeping food below 5□c does not kill the bacteria; it slows their multiplication. Freezing stops them from multiplying but does not kill them, it just leaves the bacteria dormant.

Heating: Food heated at its core to 70□c, or above, for two minutes or more will kill most bacteria.

This is why proper heating (cooking) and any subsequent re-heating is so important.

The Danger Zone

Between 5□c and 63□C bacteria multiply readily. They thrive at about 37□c. the temperature range between 5□C and 63□c is known as the "Danger Zone" because it is the temperature range at which bacteria multiply readily thereby making themselves most "dangerous".

Keep food out of the Danger Zone as much as possible!

Controlling Temperatures

Three main ways to restrict the amount of time that food is left in the Danger Zone are: □ Keep food hot, above 63□ □Keep food cold, below 5□c □ Keep food at between 5□c and 63□c for as little time as possible.

Some do's: □ Refrigerate high risk foods on delivery Thaw frozen food in a refrigerator □Keep refrigerated food stored until you need it □Cook food properly □ Serve food properly □serve food at 63□C or above □Cool hot food rapidly □ Re-heat food to above 63□C or above

Some don'ts: □Don't prepare food too far in advance of serving □ Don't thaw food insufficiently □ Don't leave food at room temperature □ Don't under cook food □ Don't cook food slowly □ Don't re-heat food at under 63□c

Temperature Guidelines

Delivery Refrigerated 0□C to 5□C

Frozen -22□c to -18□C

Storage Normal 0□C to 5□C

Refrigerated 0□c to 5□C

Frozen -

22□C to -18□C

Preparation Danger Zone For as short a time as possible.

Cooking Core Temperature At least 70□ for at least two minutes

Cooling ASA To between 10□C to 5□C in 90 minutes

Holding Short as possible Below 5□C or above 63□C

Re-heating Core temperature At least 70□C for at least two minutes

Serving Core Temperature At least 63□C

The "core temperature" is the temperature at the very centre of the food you are cooking.

Useful tools: □ Fridge and freezer thermometers □ Food temperature probe

Food Delivery Check deliveries as soon as they arrive, do not sign for them until you have checked them and are satisfied they acceptable. Use reputable supply sources.

The supplier must deliver them as safe and wholesome, fit for purpose, so if they are not, send them back- don't accept them.

Reject a food delivery if: It is perishable and delivered in the Danger Zone The packaging is damaged, dented etc. It is frozen and thawing The goods are mouldy or damaged The “use by” or “best before” date has expire

Food Storage

Storing food properly means that it is kept under the right conditions for the correct period of time.

In practice, this means: Label it on delivery Put newly delivered stock behind previous stock, use older stock first Rotate the stock so it does not go out of date Store correctly: if it needs covering, cover it; put into containers etc. Keep heavier items lower down, they are safer to move ensure nothing is stored on the floor Is ventilation adequate so food stays fresh? Is temperature low enough to keep food fresh? Is lighting adequate so staff can see what they are doing? No hot food in fridges, it makes the fridge temperatures rise Store foods that might drip underneath other foods, prevents contamination Keep fridge and freezer doors closed when not in use.

Food Preparation

Much food preparation brings the food into the Danger Zone which raises the possibility of causing food poisoning.

Some good practices when preparing food include: Keep the food area clean Maintain high standards or personal hygiene Leave the food in storage as long as possible

Thaw as slowly as possible in as cool a place as possible, Thaw completely before cooking Do not prepare the food too far in advance of its use Keep raw and cooked foods apart Touch the food as little as possible Keep food out of danger zone as much as possible. Fly screens will help keep insects out Replace kitchen light diffusers after cleaning them Make sure the electrocute is turned on.

Food Cooking

Most bacteria are killed when exposed to temperatures of 70□c or above for two minutes or more. Therefore, the hotter the food and longer it stays hot the safer the food is to eat.

Some good practices when cooking food include: □ Check the temperature at its core with a temperature probe? □ Has that temperature reached 70□c or above? □ Has the temperature been kept for two minutes or more? □ Cut large portions into smaller ones, they get hotter more quickly □ Stir soups etc. to prevent "cold spots" in the Danger Zone □Is the oven thermostat working properly? □Do you know how and when to use food temperature probes?

Food Cooling

As food cools down it has to pass through the Danger Zone. So, the faster you cool it, the less time it spends in the Danger Zone and the less likely it is to cause food poisoning.

Some good practices when cooling food include: □Aim to cool it between 10□C and 5□c within 90 minutes of cooking □ Do not put it in the fridge to do this, it might raise the fridge temperature □ Cover/ wrap the food to prevent contamination and place it in the coolest part of the food area. □ Cut larger pieces into smaller pieces, they will cool down more quickly

Food Holding

You should try to hold as little food as possible and what must be held should be done for as short a time as possible.

Some good practices when you have to hold food include: Proper labelling Maintain the temperature at the centre of the food above 63c ensure the food is handled as little as possible do not retain left overs, throw them away

Food Re-heating

Food poisoning occurs quite often as a result of food not being re-heated properly.

Some good practices when re-heating food including: Do not leave it out waiting to be re-heated, keep it cool until needed check with a probe that the food has been heated to at least 70c at its core for at least two minutes before serving Do not re-heat food more than once, throw left overs away immediately

Food Serving

Quite often, good hygiene practices are overlooked when food is being served yet this is the time when the opportunity to demonstrate good practices are reassuring to those who will be eating the food.

Some good practices when serving food include: □ Avoid leaving it standing uncovered unnecessarily □ Make sure it is served at not less than 63□c, particularly where a meal may have to be served in a person’s room by tray □ Hold cutlery and cups by their handles to avoid contamination □ Encourage people to eat as quickly yet as comfortably as possible to avoid food cooling too much and becoming exposed to contamination. □ When someone has finished eating throw away all left overs immediately □ clear up immediately □ Staff who serve food or may feed someone must be appropriately and relevantly instructed in appropriate food hygiene practices □ Keep pets out of the serving area, particularly whilst serving

Personal Hygiene

People are potential carriers of pathogenic bacteria that cause food poisoning. Therefore, we have to maintain high standards of personal hygiene to avoid contaminating food.

Skin:

Washing every day is necessary for general hygiene because bacteria live on skin. Hand is extremely important in both care work generally and food handling.

Hair

Keep it clean and tidy, tie it back and/or wear a hat to cover it when handling food. Also when you are handling food, do not touch you hair and if you do, wash your hands immediately afterwards.

Mouth, nose, ears:

Do not eat, chew or smoke when handling food because this could transfer saliva to the food (ash as well in the case of smoking) which contains bacteria that could cause food poisoning. Wash your hands before and after eating, chewing or smoking.

Wash your hands immediately after touching your face.

If you have to blow your nose, do so with paper tissue and throw it away properly, then wash your hands immediately.

Using the toilet:

Remove any food related clothing such as hat, coat, apron etc before using the toilet. Wash your hands thoroughly after using the toilet and before putting the food related clothing back on.

Toiletries etc:

Avoid strong smelling perfumes, deodorants etc. which can taint the food.

Jewellery:

Bacteria can live under straps and rings which can contaminate food. Avoid wearing jewellery when handling food. Wedding rings etc. must be covered with a blue waterproof plaster to prevent food contamination.

Clothing:

Clean and light coloured so stains show prompt cleaning

Avoid buttons that could fall into food Head covering

Flat, non-slip footwear that covers the toe and heel

Cuts and Grazes

Cover cuts, grazes, scratches, spots etc with blue waterproof dressing to prevent possible bacterial contamination of food.

Diarrhoea and Vomiting:

If you have a cold or contagious illness you must not handle food. Notify the most senior person on duty immediately who may require a medical “all clear” before you can handle food again

Hand Washing

Wash hands after:

Using the toilet touching your face you hair cleaning Handling waste Taking a rest break Handling different food Handling new food

Remember

Only use the sink specifically dedicated for hand washing

Use soap, liquid soap is better than soap bars which can harbour bacteria Use hot water Use a nail brush to clean under your nails never dry your hands with kitchen towels.

Pets and Pests

They can contaminate our food through physical contamination through saliva, droppings or urine.

Pets:

Pets must be kept away from the food handlers and the food process □ pets must never be fed in or around food areas

Rodents:

Keep food covered to prevent insects getting to the food □ Clear up spillage, this denies insects the food they want □ Put food away, do not leave it out □ Eggs and maggots are warning signs for pets □ Insect and bug nets eliminate and reduce insects problems

Birds:

Carry bacteria, keep them away from food □ always wash hands after handling birds or cleaning cages

Premises

Food premises should allow for:

Easy cleaning □ separation of clean and dirty work Safe waste disposal □ Minimum moving and handling sensible work flow □ Sufficient storage □ Good drainage □ Good Lighting □ Adequate ventilation Personal Hygiene □ Pest Control □ Separate “hand wash only” facilities □ Toilet must not lead onto food areas

Equipment

Anything you use in association with food, from a fork to a freezer, is “food equipment”

Food equipment:

Must be non-toxic Should be smooth for easy cleaning Keep in good condition Ensure it is properly maintained Take out of service if worn, damaged or faulty Where possible, choose stainless steel equipment

Work surfaces:

Ensure they are heat resistant They must be easy to clean Their condition must be good avoid cracks or joins, they can harbour bacteria Keep free of clutter that can harbour dirt and bacteria Wood is unsuitable Chopping boards should be polypropylene (plastic) Colour coded chopping boards might help

Colour Codes for Food Boards

Red – Raw meat Blue – Raw fish Yellow – Cooked meat Green – Salad and Fruits Burgundy - Vegetables

White – Baked and dairy products

Cleaning & Disinfection

Cleaning prevents food equipment and food areas from contaminating food, which includes making the food area less attractive to pests looking for food sources

Chemicals that clean are called detergents. Chemicals used for disinfecting are called disinfectants

Some chemicals combine detergents and disinfectants, they are called "sensitizers".

The less cluttered the work area, the easier is it to keep clean and disinfected.

An extremely important principal is to

"Clean as you go"

The two key elements to good cleaning are:

The way you clean □ the cleaning frequency

The way you clean

Pre-clean Scrap off food, brush up crumbs etc

Main clean Wash with hot water and detergent

Rinse Use clean hot water until detergent washed off

Disinfect Leave the disinfectant on long enough to kill bacteria

Final Rinse Use clean hot water until disinfectant is washed off

Drying If possible, leave to dry off naturally. If not, use disposable paper towel to dry off

Avoid using cloths for drying

Chemicals:

Read and follow instruction labels Never mix chemicals Use the correct amount Ensure containers are clearly marked Store them properly Wear suitable clothing Do not bring in chemicals not authorised by the manager

Dishwashers:

Kill bacteria better than hand washing because the water is hotter Follow instruction for use Service Regularly

Waste disposal:

Indoor bins – accessible but out of the way of food lids must fit properly Keep lids closed when not in use Line with a disposable liner

Outdoor bins:

Must never overflow keep clean Empty regularly

Cleaning schedule

A cleaning schedule is a written routine for what must be cleaned, when, how and by whom.

It ensures regular, systematic and. Therefore thorough cleaning that prevents anything being forgotten

SUMMARY OF FOOD SAFETY

Chartered Institute of Environmental Health

Food Safety.

The protection of consumer health and wellbeing by safeguarding food from anything that can cause harm

Contamination.

The pressure in food of any harmful or objectionable substance or object.

Food-borne illness/food poisoning.

Types of illness caused by eating contaminated food

Hazard.

Anything that could cause harm to consumers.

HACCP (Hazard Analysis and Critical Control Point).

A formal system that helps food businesses to protect food safety.

Role of enforcement officers.

Provide food safety advice.

Inspect food premises.

Enforcement legislation that releases to food.

Powers of enforcement officers.

Enter and inspect food premises.

Investigate outbreaks of food poisoning and foodborne illness and possible offences.

Remove suspect food and have it destroyed if it is considered to be unsafe to eat.

Serve improvement and prohibition notices.

Take food businesses to court for breaking food safety laws.

Food handler – legal requirements

Keep yourself clean.

Keep the workplace clean.

Protect food from contamination or anything that could cause harm.

Follow good personal hygiene practices – e.g. hand washing.

Wear appropriate protective clothing.

Tell your employer if you are suffering from or are a carrier of a food-borne illness.

Due diligence

A food business must be able to demonstrate that it has taken all reasonable precautions to prepare food that is safe to eat

Three types of hazards caused by contaminants:

Physical

Chemical

Biological

Food poisoning is caused by:

Micro-organisms:

- bacteria
- viruses
- moulds and fungi

Natural poisons in food itself

Chemicals/metals

Natural poisons

Wild Mushroom Green Potatoes Red Kidney Bean

Three types of bacteria:

Pathogenic – cause illness

□Helpful – used to make beer, cheese, yoghurt, etc.

□Spoilage – cause food to perish/rot/go mouldy

Pathogenic micro-organisms linked to food poisoning and food-borne illness:

Campylobacter jejune

Staphylococcus aureus

Bacillus Cereus

Salmonella

E.coli 0157 H7

Clostridium porringers

Norovirus

Pathogenic micro-organisms

Staphylococcus aureus, Bacillus cereus

produce toxins in food

generally accuse vomiting

quick onset

Campylobacter jejune, Salmonella, E.coli, Clostridium perfringens

originate in the gut

generally cause diarrhoea

slower onset

Binary fission

The right conditions

Food

Moisture

Warmth

Time

Spore-forming bacteria

The canning industry is based upon killing Clostridium botulinum spores by using very high temperatures

High-risk foods

Meat Pie, Cooked Chicken, Meat Lasagne and Cream Cakes

High-risk foods

Ready to eat, Moist, High in protection and require strict time and temperature control

Cross-Contamination

Raw to cooked food

Temperature measuring devices

Hard probe thermometer

Infra-red probe (gun type) thermometer

Using a temperature probe

Should be:

properly calibrated

cleaned and disinfected between use

Chilled storage

At or below:

8 degrees Celsius – law

5 degrees Celsius – good practice

Frozen storage

Wrap food to prevent:

contamination

freezer burn

Thawing food

Check to ensure that food is properly thawed before cooking

Cooking

Ensure that you cook food thoroughly

Reheating food

Reheat food to a minimum temperature of 75 degrees Celsius ONCE only

Hot holding

At or above 63 degrees Celsius

Cooking

Always check that food is cooked thoroughly

Hand washing

One of the most important actions you can take to help prevent contamination

How to wash your hands

Always use a hand basin provided exclusively for washing hands

Use comfortable hot water rub your hands vigorously to work in the soap

Don’t forget the areas in between your fingers and around your wrists

Rinse your hands before drying them

Personal Hygiene

You must maintain the highest possible standards of personal hygiene to avoid contaminating food

Preservation

Preservation methods remove one or more requirement for bacterial growth

Date marking

Use-by date on ready-to-eat foods – criminal offence to sell food past is use- by date

Best-before date-canned, dried and frozen products can be sold past best-before date but safety and quality could be compromised

Stock rotation

FIFO – 'first in first out' – the golden rule of stock rotation

Chilled storage

Clean and defrost thoroughly

Cover and label food

Keep food tidy

Don't over sock

FIFO

No warm food

Separate raw and ready material ready-to- eat foods

Decant food from metal containers

Frozen storage

Clean and defrost thoroughly

Cover and label food

Keep food tidy

Don't over stock

No warm food

FIFO

Dry goods storage

Ventilated, clean and light

Off the floor and away from walls

Stock control and checks

Designated area for returns or discarded stock

Food allergy and intolerance

Dirty premises

Detergent

Used to dissolve grease and remove dirt

Disinfectant

Used to reduce micro-organisms to safe levels

The six stages of wet cleaning

Prepare, Clean, Rinse, Disinfectant, Final rinse, Dry and Cloths

Cloths are a common source of contamination so single-use, disposable cloths are recommended

Washing facilities

Hand wash facilities with hot and cold water, soap and drying facilities

Separate food and equipment sinks with hot and cold water

Waste disposable

Bins and waste are sources of contamination

Design of premises

Designed, constructed and equipped to minimise the risk of contamination

First aid kit

The law requires businesses to have adequate and appropriate first aid equipment, facilities and personnel on site to enable first aid to be given

Pests thrive if they can find food, moisture, warmth and shelter

Food pests:

Transmit disease

Contaminate food (bodies, hair, faeces, urine, etc)

Damage the structure of premises and equipment

Pest control

Don't interfere with pest prevention measures or equipment

Act to ensure that the food you make, serve or sell is safe to eat

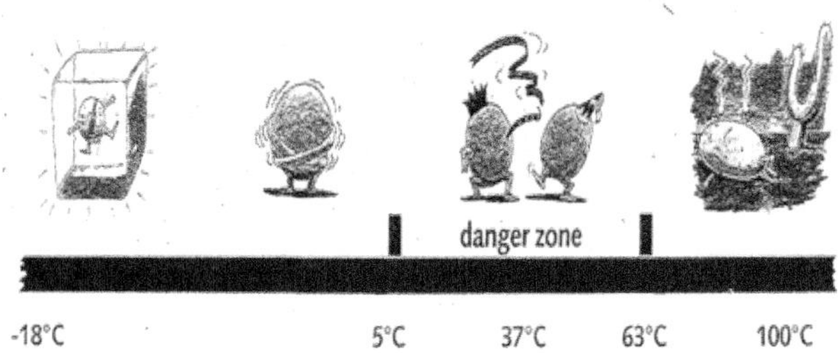

Hazard	anything in the food which could harm the consumer
Analysis	an organised step by step approach
Critical	concentrating on the most important dangers
Control	specific standards and checks to protect food safety
Point(s)	specific part(s) of the food production process

Chapter 5 Approx. page 260-288

FIRST AID

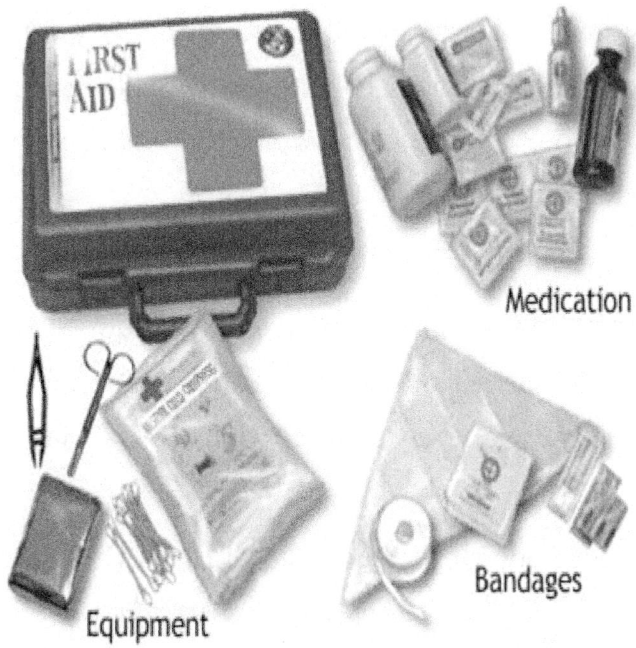

First aid Awareness

This booklet is an awareness resource, not a tool to formally train first aiders within current regulatory expectations and guidelines. Formally trained first aiders can use it as a helpful reference in supporting their formal first aid qualification. Formally trained first aiders will benefit from first aid aware colleagues if they need an extra pair of hands when dealing with a first aid situation.

First Aid Training:

You must have a formally trained first aider with a current relevant first aid certification on duty on every shift – this awareness resource will not do that for you.

Whether you opt for the First Aid at Work Course or the shorter Appointed Persons with Emergency First Aid is a matter solely at your discretion and judgement. To make this judgement, you must assess various factors which could include, for example: □ Historical problems experienced □ Probable future problems □ The nature of your service group □ Access to emergency facilities.

That training must be delivered by a suitably certificated training provider which you will find in Yellow Pages under First Aid Training.

Don’t Make Matters Worse

It is essential that, well intentioned as you might be, you do not make matters worse, therefore: Are you at risk? Do not put yourself at risk? Is the situation/area now safe itself? Who is nearby that you can use to help and/or

summon help? Do not let people crowd in, give the casualty space Protect the casualty’s personal belongings

Maintain universal infection control procedures (UICPs).

You certainly do not need any training to do any of the above.

Note: Do not give or attempt to give any first aid that you have not been formally trained and certificated to give.

This material will not give you that level of certification since this material is for awareness only.

Your intentions may be good, but we live in an environment where people are short on thanks and long on blame – they like to sue. If you do something you have not been properly trained to do and you are sued you will have an extremely expensive problem on your hands, sadly, this is the reality of the age we live in.

Priorities

Five helpful priorities to remember with regards to first aid are: Check pulse and breathing Control bleeding Immobilise bone and/or joint injuries Treat wounds SUMMON HELP!

Whilst Waiting For Help

There are some very useful things that you can do whilst waiting for help that do not require any special training, these include: Find out the casualty's name (if you do not already know it) Talk to them and reassure them, "You will be fine" Are there any obvious injuries? Try and remember any odd behaviour by the casualty How has the casualty been responding to you? Think about what has happened, try and remember it.

When help arrives, providing them with this information may save valuable time and save the casualty.

Reassure Them

Reassuring a casualty is extremely important and you do not need special training to do these 6 things:

You stay calm, consciously breathe in slowly and deeply Aim to prevent harm to anyone else Talk to the casualty, "You'll be fine" – make small talk about anything SUMMON HELP! When help arrives, tell them what you know, have found out, observed etc Protect the casualty's personal belongings, let them know you are doing so.

Remember, DO NOT do anything you have not been properly formally trained and qualified to do, even if you have seen it every week on Casualty.

Moving a Casualty

Any worker in a care environment likely to experience a casualty at work should already have had proper safe handling training – those rules apply.

A casualty should be left exactly where they were found until a suitably qualified person decides on when and how they should be moved. However, If they are clearly in imminent danger if they are not moved, different rules apply. These special circumstances could include: Drowning A building collapsing Fire (Subject to our fire policy and procedures, place of safety etc.)

A – B – C

Without oxygen, cells in the body die.

That oxygen is delivered to the cells via blood circulating around our body. Oxygen gets into the blood via our lungs as a result of breathing it in through our airway (mouth and/or nose).

So if the airway is clear, we can breathe in the oxygen for our lungs to deposit it into the bloodstream to be circulated around our body.

Hence A-B-C:

A – Airway B – Breathing C – Circulation

Airway:

The airway could become blocked by: the tongue falling back vomit dentures etc

Make sure it is clear: lift the chin tilt the head back fingers in

Breathing:

With the airway clear? does their chest move showing signs of breathing? place your cheek near their mouth, any breath? summon a qualified trained first aider immediately

To learn mouth-to-mouth resuscitation, you should attend a proper first aid training course to practice, perfect and prove knowledge of the technique.

Circulation:

To check a pulse : do not use your thumb use your index and middle fingers together use the "pads" of your fingers find the pulse on a colleague's wrist find the pulse on a colleague's neck (to the side of their wind pipe) it should beat about once every second

If circulation has failed you will need someone to administer CPR (cardiopulmonary resuscitation). To learn this, you should attend a proper first aid training course.

A-B-C is absolutely essential in first aid – it is, literally, life or death knowledge.

Recovery Position

There are many uses for the recovery position, how to do it and when are best learned on a proper first aid training course.

Accident Procedure

In any work emergency situation you must follow our accident procedure: Notify the most senior person on duty immediately The most senior person on duty takes charge Summon appropriate assistance (first aid, ambulance etc.) Reassure the person Complete accident book Notify our Inspectorate immediately If relevant, contact the HSE by calling 08453009923 (check the phone numbers) Act to prevent reoccurrence

Accident Books

Any accident whether to a person in our care, staff, visitor etc., no matter how trivial it may seem, MUST be recorded in the relevant accident book.

If the accident is to a Service User, it must be recorded in their care plan as well.

Once every month the Registered Manager will review the accident book/s taking any appropriate action.

This review will also consider staff absence to determine any correlation and need to make a report to the relevant enforcing body.

The Registered Manager will initial each entry in the accident book to show it has been reviewed and that any relevant outcomes are being managed.

Note: DO NOT initial the RIDDOR (RIDDOR (The Reporting of Injuries, Diseases and Dangerous Occurrences Regulations 2013) is a UK health and safety legislation section of the accident book unless the accident was reportable and reported under RIDDOR. Completed accident books must be kept for at least 3 years.

When we need a new accident book we contact the Health and Safety Executive on telephone number 01787881165 and

ask for a “BI 510 Accident Book” which they will send us.

Reporting of Injuries and Diseases

We recognise this as being the RIDDOR regulations which place a duty upon us to report certain injuries, diseases and dangerous occurrences.

Where a member of staff or volunteer is off work for three consecutive days or more (including days off and weekends) due to work related injury or ill health we report this to the HSE by calling 0845 300 9923.

Where someone suffers a fracture, amputation, is burnt or scalded, requires medical treatment or admission to hospital or dies due to an accident whilst in our care etc. we notify the HSE by calling 0845 300 923. We also notify our inspectorate by telephone and follow that up in writing immediately.

Any disease such as those covered by our policy on communicable diseases must be notified to the HSE by calling 0845 300 9923. We also notify our Inspectorate by telephone immediately.

After The Accident

Having dealt with the situation and followed any appropriate reporting obligations, the immediacy of the incident is over. However, it may not be entirely over, you might experience some of the following reactions: □ satisfaction □ doubt □ worry □ uncertainty □ sadness

It is possible, according to the incident, you might experience: □ shock □ sleep problems □ guilt

If any of these arise, you must tell the Registered Manager and arrange to see your doctor.

First Aid Boxes

The First Aid boxes should always contain: □ A guidance card on emergency first aid

 20 individually wrapped sterile adhesive dressing of different sizes 2 sterile eye pads

 4 individually wrapped sterile triangular bandages 6 safety pins 6 medium size individually wrapped wound dressings one pair of disposable gloves.

Universal Infection Control Procedures (UCIP)

Infection control is an important theme in good care management which extends to first aid situations as well.

There are certain methods or procedures through which we can target our control of infection in first aid situations known as universal infection control procedures, abbreviated to UICPs.

These UICPs include: hand washing clean environment decontaminating equipment personal protective equipment (PPE) – disposable gloves, aprons etc waste management managing contact with blood, body fluids etc handling sharps, dealing with needlestick handling vomit.

However, you must understand and apply infection control procedures when involved with a first aider in a first situation.

Bleeding

Bleeding could be internal and/or external, there could be blood spurting from a wound. Seeing someone bleeding can, for some people, be off putting.

If bleeding is severe, shock is likely.

What to do: □ infection control procedures apply □ summon a first aider immediately □ cover the wound □ apply pressure if necessary to stem bleeding □ raise the injured part of the body □ maybe, lie the person down.

Nose Bleeding

What to do: □ infection control procedures apply □ sit the person down □ tilt their head forwards □ they breathe through their mouth □ pinch the soft part of the nose, just below the bridge □ a dressing may be necessary to absorb blood □ stay like this, still, for 10 to 15 minutes □ if it has not stopped, start again □ when it has stopped, clean up with warm water.

If the nose bleed is severe, lasts a long time and/or is a regular problem, medical advice should be sought.

Cuts and Grazes

What to do: □ infection control procedures apply □ clean wound in cold running water □ dry it with gauze □ cover with appropriate dressing.

Fractured Bone

There are different types of fractures, all of which require hospital advice if suspected – call 999.

Symptoms could include: □ area is less mobile □ bruising □ deformity □ pain□ swelling

Hip Fracture

This should always be considered a possibility when an elderly person has fallen – follow our fallen persons procedure.

Since the fracture may not show itself for hours, even days, keep close observation of the service user: □ they might keep off one side □ their ability to walk could be reduced □ pain □ shock.

Strains and Sprains

Ligaments, muscles and tendons can be strained or sprained, symptoms include: □ bruising □ discomfort □ impairment of mobility □ pain □ swelling

What to do: □ sit or lie the person down □ summon a first aider □ apply an ice pack to relieve swelling

Ice Packs

Ice packs are useful for "taking the heat out of" a bruise, swelling, sprain etc. What to do: □ Half fill a plastic bag with ice □ wrap it in a clean tea towel □ Place the ice pack on the affected area for 10 minutes □ change the ice as necessary

Ice packs can be very helpful in reducing back pain if you put an ice pack where it hurts.

Dressings

Only apply a dressing if you have been properly trained how to, remembering:□ infection control procedures apply □ is the dressing large enough □ open the dressing □ hold the dressing only at its edges □ do not touch the wound or the edges of the wound□ place the dressing directly onto the wound, do not slide it into place □ if blood soaks the dressing, put a new one over the top of the previous dressing □ throw used dressing away in clinical waste □ remove disposable gloves, into clinical waste □ wash your hands.

Bandages

There are many uses for bandages, including: □ controlling bleeding □ securing dressings □ supporting limbs □reducing swelling.

When applying a bandage: □ infection control procedures apply □ talk to the person, reassure them □ make the person comfortable □ work where they can see you, on the injured side □ support the injured body part □ make the bandage firm without strangling circulation □ leaves toes and fingers poking out of a bandage □ tie off the bandage with a reef knot (but not on a bony area)

Checking circulation: A wrongly applied bandage could cut off circulation which is potentially dangerous. Therefore, every 15 minutes, press the skin by the bandage. If normal skin colour does not return quickly where you pressed the skin, loosen and re-tie the bandage.

Chemical Burns

Cleaning chemicals, chemicals in a shed, dishwasher products could all potentially cause chemical burns to a service user.

Symptoms: □ intense pain □discoloration □blistering □swelling

What to do:□summon a first aider □infection control procedures apply □ventilate the area □ remove the chemical, if this has not already been done □check the data sheet for emergency advice □take appropriate action

Sunburn

An elderly service user's skin may be more sensitive to the effects of the sun than another person's skin. Furthermore, their medication might increase that sensitivity.

In the first place, taking appropriate preventative action such as suitable shade, sun creams etc. is essential.

What to do:□ Summon a first aider □infection control procedures apply □sponge the area gently with cold/cool water □allow the water to evaporate off, this helps cool the skin □maybe , calamine lotion might help □could the person also be dehydrated?

Swallowed Substances

Sadly, service users swallowing a substance hazardous to their health is not uncommon, for example, swallowing:□ a chemical □cleaning agent □drugs □insect control □rodent control

Symptoms will vary according to the substance swallowed which could include: burning pain lack of consciousness vomiting nearby evidence such as an empty bottle etc.

What to do: Summon a first aider infection control procedures apply do not make them vomit remove the substance, if this has not already been done call 999 check the data sheet for emergency advice take appropriate action keep any evidence for the ambulance crew maintain their A-B-C

Drug Poisoning

A service user could be poisoned by drugs in various ways, for example: Illegal drug use Intentional overdose administration error inappropriate change in medication

Symptoms may vary and prompt action is necessary: Summon a first aider notify the most senior person on duty infection control procedures apply call 999 Keep evidence (MAR sheet, bottle etc.)

Electrocution

You may see the following symptoms if someone have been electrocuted:□Bruising □muscle spasms □they appear stunned □their heart might stop □ their breathing might stop.

Do not touch the person:□ They might be ''live'' □ you could also be electrocuted

What to do:□ Call for immediate help □ have the first aider summoned □have the power supply turned off immediately □if you cannot get the power supply stopped:- stand on a phone book- use a wooden handle to push them away from the electrical source: □ Follow our accident and emergency procedures

Heart Attack

The blood supply to the heart muscle is, for some reason, obstructed which in turn causes the heart to stop – this is known as a heart attack.

Symptoms could include:□ Severe chest pain □ that pain often spreads down one or both arms □the casualty experiences breathlessness, they often gasp for air □ lips go blue □ skin goes "Ashen" □they become sweaty, clammy □ they feel faint and/or dizzy a sudden collapse is possible

What to do:□ Summon a first aider immediately □call 999 □ sit the person up in half sitting, half lying position □prop them up with cushions, pillows etc □

loosen clothing reassure them , they will probably be very frightened

Stroke

The blood supply to the brain is, for some reason, impaired. This causes brain cells to die resulting in what is known as a stroke.

Symptoms could include : Speech difficulties difficulty swallowing sudden painful headache confusion loss of limb movement loss of consciousness

What do to? summon a first aider immediately call 999

Seizures / Fits

Due to the disturbance in the brain, body muscles move involuntarily known as seizures and/or fits which can be quite disturbing both the service user and onlookers.

Symptoms: Convulsions rigidity unconsciousness their tongue might get bitten breathing could stop

What to do: Summon a first aider immediately try to move dangerous items out of the way

 Make space around the person.

Shock

There are many causes of shock, symptoms include: Rapid pulse clammy skin

If the shock worsens, symptoms could start to include: Weakness Nausea Rapid, light breathing weak pulse What to do: Summon a first aider immediately seek medical attention

Anaphylactic Shock

Anaphylactic Shock is a severe and dangerous allergic reaction which causes: Blood pressure to drop The tongue and throat to swell.

It could be caused by: Certain drugs an insect sting some foods latex allergy (latex gloves, for example)

What to do: Summon a first aider call 999 without delay

Asthma Attack

Asthma attack is extremely unpleasant and can be frightening.

Muscles in the lungs go into spasm, the airway linings in the lungs swell up which causes them to narrow and breathing becomes extremely difficult.

What do to: Summon a first aider immediately a reliever inhaler (blue cap) might help in the early stages Call 999

A Choking Adult

Firstly if there are any obstructions in their mouth that might cause the choking, simply remove them.

If this is not the problem: Summon a first aider stand to the service user's side and slightly behind them lean the person forward, facing the ground spread your hand out flat give five firm sharp slaps between the shoulder blades.

If this fall, abdominal thrusts must be administered. To learn how to do this properly you must attend a proper first aid course and have been assessed as competent to do this. You must not administer abdominal thrusts unless you have been taught to and confirmed as competent to do so.

Vomiting and Diarrhoea

Both will cause the service user to lose body fluids which may lead to them becoming dehydrated, which in itself may cause other problems.

What to do: □ Summon the first aider □ Notify the most senior person on duty □ infection control procedures apply □ keep the service user clean □ disinfect affected areas □ have the person sip fluids, little and often

Water alone will not replace lost salts etc., the most senior person on duty must take immediate rehydration advice from the service user's doctor.

Earache

The cause of earache can be anything from being illness related, to a tooth abscess, an infection etc. It can make even the most stoic person quite miserable.

What to do: □ make the service user comfortable □ sitting up slightly can sometimes help a bit □ wrap up a warm, not hot, hot water bottle in a towel □ place the bottle and towel against the ear

Calling the doctor is a matter of judgement to be made by the most senior person on duty. However, if there is fever and or/discharge, the doctor must be called.

Diabetes

Where the body struggles to control its sugar level in the blood stream, a person's "blood sugar" may be too high. □ If it is too low, this is known as hypoglycaemia □ If it is too high, this is known as hyperglycaemia.

If the service user is a known diabetic, summon a first aider and follow care plan guidance which must involve sugar level testing and corrective guidance. Where consciousness is affected, call 999 immediately.

Hypothermia

A person's body level falls too low and can be fatal. Those who are inactive, frail etc. are more at risk than others. Symptoms include: □ cold skin □ slow breathing □ weak pulse □ shivering □ feeling disorientated

If the person is elderly, what to do: Summon a first aider □ call 999 □ get the service user wrapped up in blankets etc □ put a hat on them □ they must drink warm – not hot- drinks such as tea □ they must warm up slowly otherwise serious harm could occur

□ do not give them alcohol □ do not give them a hot water bottle

Bites and Stings

For most of us these causes no more than a sore or itchy minor swelling. However, in some cases, particularly insect stings, a severe life-threatening reaction can occur (see page 44). Mouth and throat stings can cause the airway to swell which can prevent breathing. In serious situations, what to do: □ summon first aider □ call 999 □ sit or lie the person down □ reassure them □ A-B-C

Traffic Incidents

Even without formal training there is much you can do to positively affect the outcome of a traffic incident, for example: □ park safely □ hazard lights on □ look out for safety □ look out for the safety of others □ if dark make sure you can be seen □ look out for others who might not be seen □ how can you warn/slow down/stop other traffic safely? □ put out warning triangles

if safe to do so, switch off the engines of vehicles involved □ summon help, call 999 etc. □ make safe any personal belongings of other involved, let them know this □ reassure casualties □ how can you enlist others to get involved in these things

USE DRABC

DANGER Before attempt to give first aid, make sure that both you and patient are safe environment

RESPONSE; quick check if the patient is conscious

AIRWAY; check if the airway is clear

BREATHING; check the breathing

CIRCULATION; check any bleeding and patient alive

SURVEYs

PRIMARY; survey which is the priority assessment

SECONDARY; is to gather all information include; the patient conscious level

Be systematically

Keep good record in order to hand over to ambulance

- **Direct pressure**
- **Elevation**
- **Lay down**

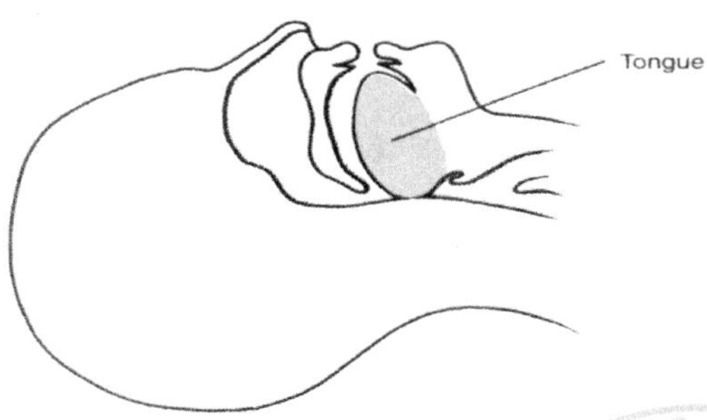

Choking

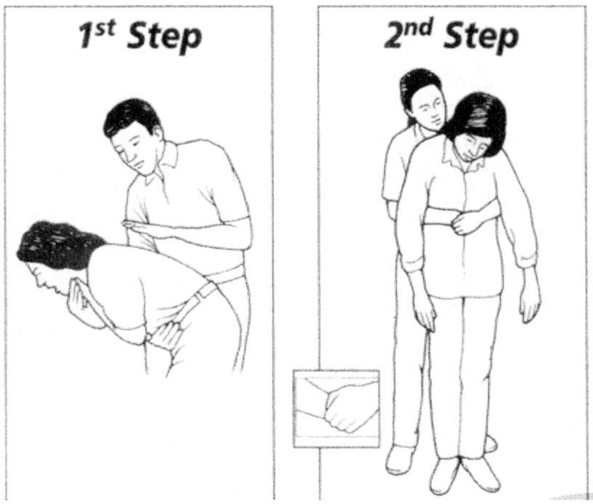

RECOVERY POSITION

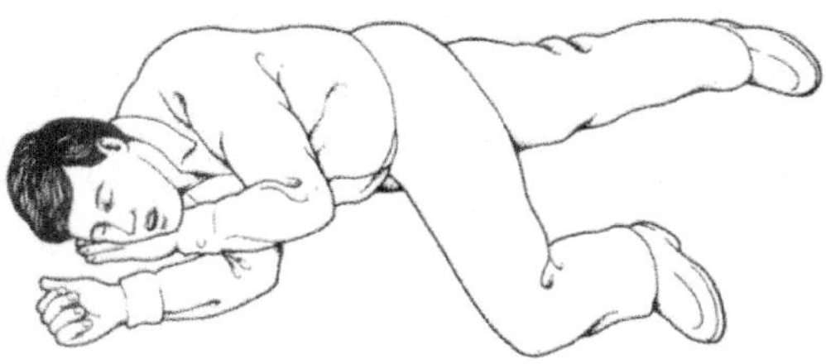

Treatment

Aim:	*Urgent hospital treatment*
Action:	*Get help – ambulance* *Casualty to self-medicate (epinephrine)*
Position if conscious:	 *To ease breathing*
Position if unconscious:	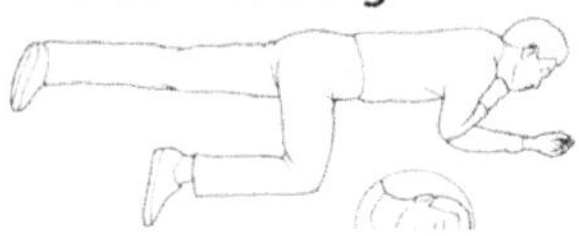

Chapter 6 Approx.. Pages 289-298

MANUAL HANDLING

More than one third of all-over three-day injuries reported each year to the Health and safety executive are caused by Manual handling the transporting or supporting of loads by hand or by bodily force. As per the Manual Handling Regulations 1992, the staff must follow the individual client's manual handling risk assessments and use designated equipment.

Employers Duties Will:

Avoid the need for hazardous manual handling as far as it is reasonably practicable.

Assess the risk of injury.

Reduce the risk of injury as is reasonably practicable by providing equipment.

Employees also have duties to;

Follow correct procedures, as per individual Manual Handling Risk Assessment.
Use equipment as instructed.
Co-operate with employer.
Inform employer if they identify hazardous handling activities.

Take care to ensure they do not put others at risk.

Participate in manual handling training.

Assessing the risk

The Home will carry out individual risk assessments, which are recorded on manual handling and will ensure all staff read and implement procedures.

Risks will be reduced to the minimal levels as practicable. Staff are to familiarize themselves with the following lifting techniques if lifting equipment is identified as being needed. Staff must only use the equipment once they have been trained as being competent to do so.

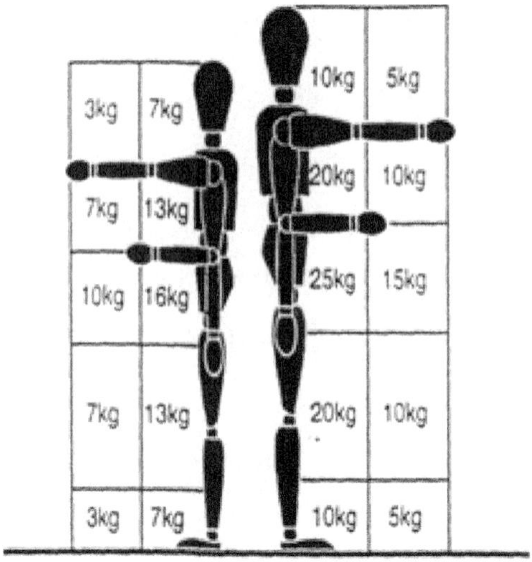

Each box in the diagram above shows guideline weights for lifting and lowering

Observe the activity and compare to the diagram. If the lifter's hands enters more than one box during the operation, use the smallest weight.

Use an in-between weight if the hands are close to a boundary between boxes.

If the operation must take place with the hands beyond the boxes, make a more detailed assessment.

The weights assume that the load is readily grasped with both hands.

The operation takes place in unreasonable working conditions with the lifter in a stable body position.

Operation involving more than twice the guideline weights should be rigorously assessed even for very fit, well-trained individuals working under favourable condition.

There is no such thing as a completely “safe” manual handling operation, but working within the guidelines will cut the risk and reduce the need for a more detailed assessment.

Good handling

technique

Here are some important points, using a basic lifting operation as an example

Plan the lift Where is m

the load to be placed7 IU

' !se appropriate handling *^ aids if possible Do you need help with the load? Remove obstructions such as discarded wrapping materials. For a long lift, such as floor to shoulder height, consider resting the load mid-way on a table or bench to change grip

Stop and think

Position the feet

Feet apart, giving a balanced and stable base for lifting (tight skirts and unsuitable footwear make this difficult) leading leg as far forward as is importable and if possible, pointing in the first Linn yarn intend to

Adopt a good posture

When lifting from a low level, bend the knees. But do not kneel or over flex the knees. Keep the back straight, maintaining its natural curve (tucking in the chin helps). Lean forward a little over the load if necessary to get a good grip. Keep the shoulders level and facing in the same direction as the hips.

Get a firm grip

Try to keep the arms within the boundary formed by the legs. The best position and type of grip depends on the circumstances and individual preference;

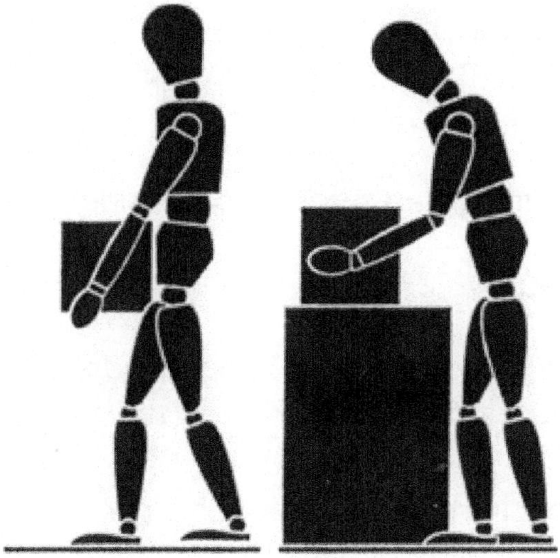

A hook grip is less tiring than keeping the fingers straight. If you need to vary the grip as

Keep close to the load

Keep the load close to the trunk for as long as possible Keep heaviest side of the load next to the trunk. If a close approach to the load is not possible, slide it towards you before trying to lift

Don't jerk

Lift smoothly, raising the chin as the lift begins, keeping control of the load.

Position the feet

Don't twist the trunk when turning to the side.

Put down and adjust

If precise positioning of the load is necessary, put it down first, then slide it into the desired position

How do one know if there is a risk of harm?

It's a matter of judgement in each case, but there are certain things to look out for. such as people puffing and sweating, excessive fatigue, bad posture, cramped work areas, awkward or heavy loads or a history of back troubles. Operators can often highlight which activities are unpopular, difficult or arduous.

There is no such thing as a completely 'safe' manual handling operation. It's difficult to be precise: so many factors vary between jobs, workplaces and people. But the general risk assessment guidelines filter (see section 9) should help to identify when a more detailed risk assessment is necessary. Working within the guidelines will reduce the need for a more detailed risk assessment.

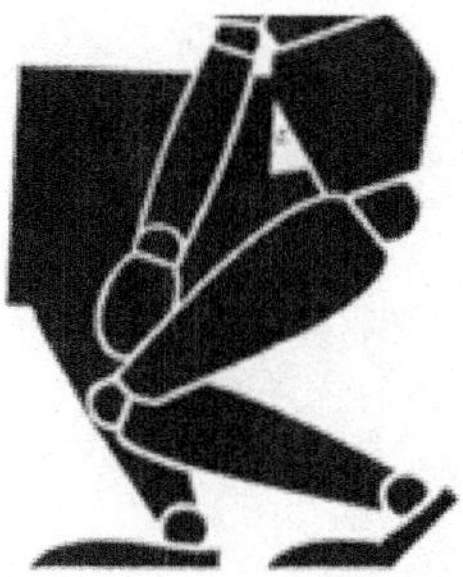

the lift proceeds, do it as

smoothly as possible.

Chapter 7 Approx. page 299-399

Health and Safety

Questions and Answers

1) **Q;** Describe the role of the supervisor in accident prevention?

A; There are many roles for the supervisor as he\she is the responsibility of the whole operation in the work place. The role of accident prevention superior is a very important as he\she controls the work that is being completed by the employee and this plays an important part towards the accident. The superior or foreman is directly involved in the day to day running, and he or she is the key the key person as he\she would understand the safe method of working and they would be capable of being capable of being able to communicate efficiently with the work force to motivate and corrects others. The supervisor ~just be adequately trained for the job in hand and have the confidence to train new employee in the philosophy that safety comes first. The supervisor must demonstrate to all employees that there is safe working way to achieve any without accidents. And quickly stop those who think otherwise and demonstrate to them where they are going wrong in polite manner.

2) **Q;** Write notes on factors that could Couse employee to commit unsafe acts in the workplace.

A; Unfortunately there are those in the work force that turn to make mistakes and unknowingly may cause accident at their place of work. The reason that these so-called accidents happen are many and some are deliberate. Deliberate action made by a disgruntled employee, do happen, however not often and some unsafe acts happen due to stress.

3) **Q;** How does stress affect employee?

A; Stress in working place affect employees, some of the reasons being

Working with bad altitude, not efficiently trained for that particular position.

That the employee find that he\she is physically unsuitable.

However stress in a family life can affect this or he\she work performance and therefore bringing more stress in a work place

4) **Q;** How many parties involved in accidents prevention at work?

A: There are two main parties involve in accident prevention are primarily the employer who is responsible for safe working condition and the employee who is responsible for safe work.

5) **Q**; Name some third party and equipment that could contribute to accident at work?

A; However accidents prevention goes a lot deeper, for example the engineer who designs the machine with the emergency stop control. The safety guards and rails.

The architect that designs the building for that machine and works out what type of floor will that machine will sit on.

The electrician will provide the suitable lighting for that particular machine Accident prevention is the responsible for everyone.

6) **Q;** what is good house keeping

A: Good housekeeping is a vital daily task in any business.

7) **Q;** Who is responsible for good housekeeping?

and it is the responsibility of both employee and the employer, to make sure that the duty of good housekeeping is achieved on the daily basis. It is the responsibility of employees and employers

8) **Q**: What is the aim and objective of good housekeeping?

A; The aim and objective of good housekeeping is to provide pleasant working condition, will improve efficiency, effectiveness, and economic. With Appling good housekeeping, there are many benefits that come in long term. These can be achieve by the employee, cleaning their working area, put rubbish into the bins provided, putting tools away, and keeping workdays and emergency exit clear of any debris. Benefit reduce fire hazards, increase employee moral increase production

The arrangement of the workplace must be tidy, and equipment is arranged in systematic to make it easier to locate items or equipment as per health and safety regulation must be adhering to without any compromise.

9) **Q;** Explain Good house keeping

A; One way of making a safe working environment is to start with good housekeeping which can be achieved by including and encouraging employee to put away tools and equipment after use, to keep their area of work clean and tidy by placing rubbish and debris in the bins provided which will help to reduce the risk of fire., keep walkways clear of debris and trip hazards, and keep emergency exists clear from Obstruction. Housekeeping improve working environment, reduce risk of accident and moral boaster for both employee and employers conservation of material and parts.

10)**Q**: what is the benefit of good housekeeping?.

Good housekeeping will reduce accident such as article dropping from above to employee head, greasy and dirty floors will cause slipping, and cause employee being injured on projecting items example nails. Conservation of material, using space available wisely.

11)**Q**: What is the benefit of doing things in orderliness manner

There must always be orderliness in the workplace. Order is the first step in doing anything right. A programme of orderliness earned out by supervision and individual employees, can bring large reductions in accidents, stores inventories, and wasted time and energy. The end result of order is greater and safer production of better products at lower costs. Improved production and costs mean increased business and prosperity for any organisation and its employees

12)**Q**; What difference altitude of employee who work in clean environment and one in dirty?

The worker who spends eight hours or more in a clean, cheerful and comfortable working environment is likely to have a different outlook from one who is forced to exert himself in a drab, dirty, or uncomfortable environment. Quite apart from any attendant losses in efficiency, anything less than desirable for the physical environment is indefensible on broader grounds.

13)**Q;** What are important issue to have in the environment?

A: Environment must have adequate light, ventilation and hazard free such as asks, roadways and passage clearly identify, order material when needed and avoid stockpiling, use FIFO (first come first out. Staff must be trained for specific task and information display on staff notice board.

14) **Q;** Why are special precaution needed for health and Safety?

A; It will promote safety and efficient operation of the organization

Special precaution must be taken, with the use and storage of substances like liquids and chemicals, and with tools and equipment, particularly explosive, power tools for example, "Hilti guns" which is a power tools that with the use of explosive cartridge can drive, special nails into concrete or drive self-tabbing bolt into steel. These types of tools must be stored under lock and key when is not being used, do not allow untrained employee to use it.

15) **Q;** How are liquid and chemical stored?
A: With the use of storage of liquid and chemicals. guidance should be sought from the manufacture as to the use and storage of such liquids and chemical as they must show the hazard of that particular substance

Chemicals such as chlorates, nitrates and peroxides can become explosive if mixed or come in contact with organic substance. Liquid and chemicals must be used a well-ventilated area by a suitable employee who would have knowledge of COSHH (control of substance Hazardous to Health).

Avoid agents such as chlorate, nitrate peroxide, being mixed improperly or coming in contact with resin, stanch to avoid explosion.

16) **Q:** When are faulty circuits a factor?
A; Faulty circuit becomes a factor when electrical circuits become overloaded. The overloading can produce localize heating of conductors this heat generated can be so great that it may ignite nearby flammable material and cause a fire. Also the heating of these over loaded conductors may cause a deterioration of insulating materials used this may also cause a fire. In a case the insulating material must be replaced with a new substance of insulated material and tested by a qualified person toughly before resuming operation.

17) **Q**: What safety precautions should be taken?
A: A manager or supervisor must ensure that all precautions are taken to prevent fires by training himself or herself to recognise any fire hazards. A regular inspection of the premises making sure that if any hazards are recognised collective action is immediately taken to prevent a fire starting in the first place as the following could be a potential fire hazard;

18) **Q:** Name some issues that employee be trained?

A:

1) The gathering of non -collected flammable rubbish.

2) Discard cigarette ends in metal bins

3) Portable heaters placed near combustible materials or liquids.

4) "Low flash point "flammable liquids stored incorrectly'.

5) Oxygen and propane\acetylenes lines not clearly marked.

6) Inappropriate fire extinguishers for the job in hand.

7 Incorrect pneumatic fittings which inadvertently will connect to oxygen and propane\acetylene lines.

8 Unmarked or blocked emergency exits.

9 Smoking near where flammable liquids are used or stored.

10 The incorrect use \storage of hazardous chemicals.

11 Avoid overloading wall socket

12 Switch of electric appliance when not in use

13 Competent persons to carry out work which result sparks example cutting or welding or hot work, avoid flammable liquid

Avoid oil-soaked rags lying around to prevent spontaneous combustion

19)**Q:** Explain what preventive measures should be taken?

A: There are a number of preventive measures that can be considered, that employers and employee should be able to recognise the main cause of fire whether it is class 3 (electric) or class 1 (wood \paper) and by holding a regular safety meeting, staff can be taught what fire extinguishers are suitable to use and on which type of fire.

20)**Q;** How should chemical be used?

Chemicals must be used in well ventilated areas as a build-up of flammable and toxic fumes can be ignited by a single spark.

Chemicals must be used as per the manufacturer's instructions and spillages must be avoided. There must be good ventilation and adequate light.

Chemicals must never be stored in open containers and in a ventilated area.

21)**Q:** what precaution on electric and tools use?
A: All electrical power outlets must be switch off when any electrical equipment is not in use.

All tools and equipment must be correctly stored when not in use.

22) **Q;** which area that no smoking sign is a must?
A: Install No smoking signs especially flammable hazards (gases, vapour, liquid, also it is advisable to mark, and unblocked fire exist. Staircases and passages must be constructed for easy exit, place fire extinguishers near fire hazards.

23) **Q;** What is risk assessment?
A; Risk Assessment - A process used to decide on priorities and to set objectives for eliminating hazards and reducing risks.

24)**Q**: What is safe systems of work?
Safe Systems of Work - How we work the likelihood that harm may occur k or expect to carry out our work

in a safe manner (avoid taking short-cuts Protect others against Health and Safety risks from work activities.

Provide safe means of entry and exit.

Provide a safe working environment.

Provide safe plant and equipment.

Provide safe systems of work.

25) **Q;** Where is the motivation important?
A: Employers should motivate their employees to a ruling that safety comes first. Regular weekly or monthly meetings should be held so that an appropriate person, manager\supervisor to explain the employees that it the interest of all that safety must come first. Motivation is very important key in this matter because if employees are not motivated and kept up to date with any changes, for example, changes in machinery, changes in the materials or changes in working practices, then accidents may be unavoidable

26) **Q** :briefly outline the major causes of fires at the workplace?
A: The major causes of fires in the workplace are; Untrained employee.

Faulty electrics cause by overloading socket.2) Open flames example the burning of rubbish.3) Hearted surfaces e.g. surface that had just been welded.4) Matches, lighters and cigarettes.5) Spontaneous ignition (combustion) 6) Chemical reaction.7) Static electricity. Fiction.8) Sparks cutting tools or welding. 9) Temporary wiring, cables, wire under carpet, 10) unattended switch on electric appliances 11) Flammable liquid, 12) Arson avoid element that cause fire

Mains voltage; this is the common voltage in domestic premises and workplaces, normally taken from 3-pin socket points and usually supplied between 220v & 240v.

27)**Q;** List five reasons why in certain instances protective equipment and clothing is not worn?

A; The five reasons are

1 The employee is not challenge or discipline for their disregard for not wearing or using protective equipment.

2) The employee does not understand the dangers for not wearing and using protective clothing and equipment.

3) The equipment and clothing cannot be comfortable worn with ease.

2) The equipment and clothing interferes with normal working duties

The employee has not been trained and had not proper induction to his working environment

28) **Q;** Write short notes on six health hazards detrimental to the health of workers?.

A: Six health hazards detrimental to employee health include;

1) Vibration such as long-term use of machines and equipment giving resulting vibrations with effect an employee's health, example back pain joint pain fingers.

2) Noise such as, too much noise can lead to headaches, loss of

hearing, tinnitus, could eventually lead to total deafness which will affect the person ability to in workplace and their health.

3) Skin Irritants, example radiation bacteria and abrasion, parasites, friction, poi sonic plant

4) Air pollution such as asbestos, smoke, toxic fumes, dust

5) Illumination, in the working environment dangerous accident do happen, an employee can be run over or crushed by a machine. The employee is not able to perform to the standard and hence can cause accident.

6) Uncomfortable temperature (too hot or too cold)

Q: organs such as lungs, heart, circulation system, hearing, sight and smell It is very

29)**Q:**What is the aim of using PPE

The aim of using protective clothing and equipment is to protect the human body and all its senses, e.g., hearing, sight and smell, from harm. Workers who do not wear goggles or earmuffs could lose their sight or sense of hearing. Workers should also be protected from the stealthy killers such as asbestos dust, imperceptible gases, e.g., LPG or liquefied petroleum gases, and mercury poisoning. Gases and other harmful substances should be correctly stored in properly marked containers. Employers should always monitor the levels of poisonous gases and other dangerous substances in their factories.

Because every injury on duty has financial implications for both the employer and the employee, it is essential that injuries should be reduced to the absolute minimum. Workmen who are injured on duty can often claim for compensation in terms of the Health and Safety Act. In general no compensation is paid if the workman is guilty of serious and wilful misconduct. Any compensation is paid from public liability insurance which any employer must have.

30) **Q:** What is the requirements for protective clothing and equipment?

As far as personal protective clothing and equipment are concerned, the worker must be able to wear the equipment with ease and comfort; the protective clothing or equipment must not interfere with his normal working procedures; the necessity for wearing protective clothing/equipment must be brought home to the worker; and economic and other disciplinary action must be used to coerce the worker to constantly use protective clothing and equipment.

The problem encountered with protective clothing and equipment is the fact that these measures do not eradicate the danger of mechanical hazards of machinery - these hazards have to be designed out of machinery; the correct choice of equipment is not always easy; and getting workers accustomed to protective gear is sometimes difficult.

31)**Q:** Name some (PPE) types of physical protective equipment available

Besides respirators and masks to filter out dust and fumes, and goggles and shields to guard the eyes, the following protective equipment is available:

Protective hard hats/caps;

Nets for long hair;

Aprons, suits and jackets;

Earmuffs;

Visors and face shields;

Welding helmets;

Boiler suits;

Dustcoats;

Safety boots and smelter boots;

Spats and leggings;

Air-suits for radiation and chemical protection;

Gloves and mittens; and

Safety shoes.

32) **Q**; What is PPE made from?

Protective garments can be made of plastic, leather, artificial fibres and so forth, depending on what type of protection is desired.

33) **Q;** Why is it important to protect external skin?

A: It is important to protect human external (skin-head hair) and internal important to use protective clothing and equipment PPE such as had hats\caps, nets, aprons, face shields, welding helmet, ear buffs, boiler suit, dust-

34) **Q;** Give example of law

A: It is the law of the country under the health and safety Act, Example if someone is working in oil refinery, the employee must use the personal protective equipment to avoid damage to the skin or eyes.

35) **Q;** What PPE are used for people working in dangerous environment?

A: Some work required wearing of a hard hat to protect the individual from falling object, use fire retardant overall to protect employee from hot pipe network, protect the feet with steel toe caped, use groves to protect your hands, safety glasses or over glasses to protect your eyes from dust and sparks, ear protection example working in very noisy area.

Welder uses a face shield with smoked glass to protect their eyes from the glare from the arc welding. Thick gauntlets to protect their hands and in some cases leather apron or jacket or trousers to protect body parts from burned.

36) **Q;** Who supply PPE at work?

A: Personal protection equipment must be supplied by the employer and the employee must use and wear such equipment if called upon to do so.

37) **Q:** What happen if employee have accident at work?

A; If an employee has an accident and was found that they were not using or wearing personal protection equipment they will have to not only suffer from any injuries, but may be prosecuted under the health and safety act, lose their job and suffer the financial burden of maybe paying a fine or imprisonment.

38) **Q;** Will PPE give total protection from injury?

No, example When a steel fixer, scaffolders and Riggers are working on height, they are required to wear a safety harness, although this will not stop them from falling, It will stop them falling to far and hitting the ground and therefore protecting them from serious injury.

39) **Q**; What would occur if there was a lack of management control?

A; If there were a lack of management control, there would be too many losses, confusion and down grading of incidents and other related problems.

Managers and supervisors have an important part to play where safety and loss control is concerned.

They are responsible in a preventive role to rule out incidents before they occur, such as caring a risk assessment before operation begins.

Employee will not have a support to implement strategic practises. Policies may not be determined, and executive's control of accident prevention thus increases cost, reduce quality and production. There will be lack of induction; discipline loss of staff moral equipment may not be checked for safety PPE may not be used properly. Risk of health and safety officer put restriction prohibition or closes business if serious accident occurs,

40) **Q;** why should an accident prevention programme start with top management?

A; The reason accident prevention programs must start with top management include it is reassuring that top management support prevention programme.

Because only top management have the authority to produce and implement polices

Management must quickly reduce injuries and introduce accident prevention as an important part of any operations.

Accident prevention must be constant reminded to all managers' supervisors and all other employees along with such matters as cost quality and production.

Need to appreciate cost of safety, health and safety and to manage training.

41)**Q;** Clearly define organisational policy.?

A: This is description of all of the organisation's policies and procedure that can be used as a useful point of reference and should be made essentially clear, as required, in any effort in loss control programme. It is fundamental or focal point to fall back on, especially in control programming.

42) **Q;** Clearly Delineated Standards for management work.

A; This means that the need to identify, out line and document, with an explanation of the standards required for each level of management. The document can vary in size from complete manuals to a brief booklet with a few chosen words describing the responsibilities of management regardless the degree of difficult wording or detailed explanation for any and all operation carried out by the organisation.

43) **Q**; Evaluate individual performance

A: This means that the organisation may examine an individual member to see how well their performance is, for example, a person's efficiency and productivity. It helps an organisation to choose with product or practices to continue or stop depend on the demand or profitability

44) **Q;** Why is use of self-appraisals important?

A; Some organisations require individuals to a self-appraisal of their degree of efficiency in their area of profit and loss control. Some of the appraisal could be bias; however, this evaluation may lead to self-improvement. And as a tool for morale booster or need to improve the specific task

45)**Q;** Explain measurement of control

A: Most large organisation with loss control programmes will throughout a certain length of time, for example, monthly quarterly, or yearly will have an organise "audit". This is to measure the amount of gain or loss of each section of the department of an organisation. It is good practice to have an internal auditor and to have external auditor who is independence once a year or the frequency depend on how big the organisation.

46)**Q;** Fully describe the aims of a safety training programme

A:

1. The aim of safety training programme include to prevent accident and to promote safety in all levels

2. To ensure that there are safe methods of work for all employee and employer.

3. To identify and enforce and improve safe working behaviour.

4. To bring possible hazards to light and to prevent it.

5. To make sure that training is precise and thorough

6. To give explanation why personal protection equipment is vitally important.

7. To describe why there is safety guards on machinery and to explain to correct use of machinery.

8. For employee to ask safety relate question.

Training must start with induction and refresher for existing employee.

A safety programme usually take place upon and update of the programme can updated during “toolbox”, the installation of a require piece of machinery.

47) **Q** what is safety committee’s function?
A; A safety committee’s function include

1.Eliminate physical hazards.

2.Plan and promote safety training

3.Apply disciplinary procedures.

4.Dispose of specific problems

5.Pass on specific recommendations.

6.Investigate accidents

7.Study and record accidents.

8.Organise safety competitions

48) **Q;** Describe your understanding of Disaster? Disaster can be view as unexpected incident, difficult to control which then lead to loss of example life.

In Collins Enlist dictionary (thesaurus (sixth edition 20080) the word disaster is described as a catastrophe or a failure of some kind, A disaster in my mind means a bad turn of events has happened or can happen or event turn to worse.

49)**Q;** What should safety committee promote?

A: Safety committees should not only protect employee against accident in a workplace, they should also promote a good working environment by supplying health related information to avoid illnesses in the work place, which will interrupt output and have financial implication for the organisation

50) **Q**; Give an example of disaster

A; it could be manmade, for example, a chemical spill or a road traffic collision. It could also a natural, for example a winter storm, lighting strike or a flood.

Or it could be initiated such as arson, riot, civil disturbance, football hooligans

51) **Q;** Name two important points to remember when coping with an emergency and explain why you have chosen these two points in particular.

A; Raise the alarm as quickly as is humanly possible. The sooner attention is made, the sooner help will come, as lives may depend on how quickly person action to obtain expert to the disaster area.

Evaluate all person involved. By doing this you are preventing injury or loss of life. Make sure the doors are shut after you evacuate human and pets.

52) **Q;** List five steps you should take upon finding a fire in a building.

A;

1) Raise the alarm by breaking the grass and phone emergency number for the fire brigade.

2) Evacuate the building and count them to make sure everyone and pet is safe.

Close doors behind you especially inter- leading doors

4) Once you are outside do not attempt to re-enter the building

5) Only fight a fire if you think you are competent to do so and use appropriate extinguished

53)**Q;** Why children should be wrapped in a blanket during a fire.

A: In case of fire, children should be wrapped in a blanket to protect them from fire and extreme heat it al act as insulator and prevent dehydration

54)**Q**; What is emergency manual?

A: An emergency manual is the organization/s policy of what to do in case of an emergency the manual should contain

55) **Q;** List the content of an emergency manual and explain why you feel they are an important part of the manual

A:

1) A description of possible disasters with policy and risk statements. For example, what to do in case of fire, who to contact, emergency numbers and the safe method of evacuation.

2) A description of what type of plant \factory warning system. For example, some plant may not be

run on electricity but a flammable fuel instead and may have to be shut down independently. Also, the type of warning system as there may not be any back up system.

3) A detail map of the office, plant or store. So regardless the emergency, an escape route can be achieved

4) A posted list of emergency services and telephone numbers. This is for all employees to know who to contact in any case of emergency.

5) The order and the route of evacuation, depending on the type of emergency. On an oil refinery there are more than several disasters that can happen, and each have a specific way of evacuation, for example, an escape of a poisonous gas like hydrogen sulphide (H2S) a person should evacuate either against the wind or at 90 degree to it

6) A list of key personnel and their deputies. This is for that key personnel can be informed in case of an emergency as that particular person may be the only one that has specific knowledge of the area that has the emergency in.

56)**Q;** What is Civil Defence Legislation?

A; This unite covers Civil defence act 1948, specifically civil protection 1986 chapter 22. It covers function of various authorities and resources available in case of emergencies or disaster include (CCS) civil contingencies secretariat (in cabinet) give the reason and the aim and objective of CCS.

57) **Q**; Name some issues it covers?

A; It covers how to minimise effect of natural or man-made disaster including with bomb threat (routine).

The unit also covers employee's liability insurance and labour matters,

In most cases registration is introduced to prevent similar disaster. The media plays major part.

58) **Q**; What are the two civil legislation?

A; Civil defence legislation was introduce by government and is covered by law under section 2 of the civil defence Act 1948 and also The civil protection and peace time Act 1986 Both the two of the civil defence Act covers the responsibility of the central government and the local authorities.

59) **Q;** What and why was civil contingence secretariat (CCS) form?

A; With the government a board was set up called the Civil contingence secretariat (CCS).and it report direct to the prime minister through the security, intelligence co coordinator and the permanent secretary to the cabinet office. The CCS was setting up to improve the flexibility of the central government and UK in crisis. The CCS was set up in July 2001 after the fuel crisis and the winter flood in 2000 and the foot and mouth outbreak in 2001.

60) **Q;** What is local authorities responsibilities in CCS

A: Regarding the responsibility of the local authorities in Civil Defence is to take appropriate action in case of emergency. An emergency or disaster involving destruction of properties or a damager to life or the environment can spring any local authority to act ,for example, when an oil tanker at sea runs ground and leak tons of crude oil causing not only destruction to the properties or danger to life, but environmental disaster as well.

61) **Q;** What prompted enaction of civil protection and Peace act?

A; Before the civil protection and peace time Act 1986 were introduced, there was a disaster in the village in Wales, “the Aberfan disaster was a catastrophic collapse of colliery spoil tip in the Welsh village of Aberfan, near Merthyr Tydfil on

21 \10\1966,killing 116 children and 28 adult refs(http\\en.wikipedia.org\wik\Aberfan

disaster page 7th July 2014.

62) **Q:** Summarise the Aberfan disaster?
A; Hundreds of miners getting to Aberfan, especially from the nearby Merthyr Vale Colliery as miners from Deep Navigation Colliery and Taff Merthyr Colliery in the neighbouring Taff Barged Valley, and also from pits across the south Wales coalfield. (http\\en.wikpedia.org\wiki\Aberfan disaster. Page 3,7th July 2014.

Also as the miners getting to Aberfan, there was a growing crowd of untrained volunteers who were hampering to rescue work effort being done by rescue teams that were there arriving to the area. This was a disaster to south Wales that still bring tears to my eyes today. Yet if there was more cooperation between the National coal board (NCB) and the local authorities in the Aberfan area with the planning and maintenance of the spoil tips then may be the Aberfan disaster had have never had happened.

63) **Q;** Describe the sea Express oil spill?

A: "The sea Empress" oil spill occurred at the entrance to Milford Haven Waterway in Pembrokeshire. Wales on 15th February 1996.The sea Empress was on-route to Texaco oil refinery near Pembroke when she became grounded on mid-channel rocks at Saint Ann's Head. Over the course of the week, spilled 72,000 tons of crude oil into the sea. The spill occurred between Pembrokeshire Coast National Park-one of Europe's most important and sensitive wild wife and marine conservation area. It was Britain third largest oil spillage and the twelfth largest in the world at that time (http\\en.wikpedia.org\wiki. Sea-Empress pill, page 1 7th jolly 2014).

64) **Q;** What was the impact of the environment as result of Sea Express?

A: The environmental impact was huge as birds out at sea were hit very hard during the early weeks of the spill, resulting in thousands of deaths. More damage was course to shorelines affected by bulk oil. Shore dead weed and invertebrates were killed in large quantities Mass stranding of cockles and other shellfish occurred on sandy beaches. There was an immediate ban on fishing off the coast of

Pembrokeshire and Carmarthenshire which had a devastating economic impact on the local fishing industry ”(http:\\en.wikipedia.org\wiki.Sea-Empress oil spill Page 2 7th July 2017).21

65)**Q:** How was the Sea express disaster dealt with? A; A large clean-up operation began as soon as soon as the sea empress started to spilling oil. The local authorities spilled suction tankers, pressure washers, oil absorbing scrubbers and manpower. Near one thousand people worked day and night during the disaster. The total cost of the clean-up operation, including the economic and environmental cost was estimated at 120million pounds sterling (http: Wen.wikipedia. org\wiki. Sea Empress oil- spill. Page 3 7th July 2014.)

In conclusion, the nature and extent of Civil defence mechanisms in United Kingdom was covered.

66) **Q;** List five important aspects that an organisation should established to minimise effect of a “disaster? Explain these points

A: In order to minimise the effect of a disaster an organisation should include the following important aspects.

1) Establish warning and alert system...example, on Pembroke oil refinery continues alarm will sound in case of fire. In case of gas leak, the alarm will be intermittent blast from the alarm. This must be tested at least once a week.

2) Establish an emergency evacuation route. The employee and employer must be fully aware of this upon induction and sign posted within the organisation.

3) Appoint evacuation wardens. The wardens must have excellent knowledge and experience of the evacuation routes.

4) Establish emergency rescue teams. The leader of this must be knowledgeable and very experience of how to use rescue techniques and knowledge of the premises and first aid

5) Establish standby communication system and operators. Mobile radio two-way communication systems are widely used on oil refineries; however, hand signals are also used by trade contractors, for example riggers, scaffolders and steel erecters.

67) **Q;** Explain your approach to a bomb threat.

If you find a suspicious parcel, do not torch, tell those around and alert the emergency telephone number. If you are inside a building,

1) Open as many windows as it can to minimise the damage created by a sudden rise in air pressure if an explosion happens

2) Collect boxes or bags that belong to me so that they cannot be confused with the suspected package.

3) Leave the premises by the shortest route possible and only use the stairs not the lift

4) When I have left the building to report the location of the suspect package to the police or the bomb disposal team.

5) DO NOT re-enter the building until I have proper information that it is clear to do so.

68)Q; what safety report for board of directors

A: This report will demonstrate to the board of directors that owe company is friendly, caring health and efficient environmental that prides on caring out any operations put on it by the board of directors, safety and efficiently.

69) Q; What should mission statement of organisation on Safety issues be?

A: The mission statement of the company on safety issue will be "if safety matters to you go no further" the report will highlight on the job health measure, Alcohol and Drugs, loss control of programme, programme for injury prevention, First aid, healthy competition, good physical condition, health care approach, health risks, personnel Cafeteria.

70) Q; How is on the job health measures?

The company employee are mainly local and most of them use used the local health centre which is located 300 meters from our company. It is well staffed with three doctors and five registered nurses and it available to us, in case of emergency.

We pride ourselves in keeping all employees informed on all industrial health hazards that are relevant to our operation. There are notice boards place throughout the company with information and we hold regular "Toolbox "talks where our employee are inform with any relevant information and this gives us feedback regarding our operations. Also on the notice boards is information promoting healthy lifestyles and on private health issues and where any employee can seek help.

71)_Q; What must alcohol and drugs in the report state?

A; As per the Board of director's instructions, there is a zero-tolerance concerning the abuse of any type of drugs or alcohol and this is clearly displays on all boards. It is also included as part of our induction process. Employees are well aware that they may have to provide a urine sample for testing if requested, failure to do so can bring disciplinary procedure against them...Any employee who provide a positive test is instantly dismissed without notice and may inform the police,

72) Q: Explain loss of control programmed?

A: The loss control programme is designed to lessen any interruption\disruption of services and work and is in constant implementation. We have a system employee report and take part in preventing and health or safety risk which includes personnel hygiene\cleanliness nutrition, rest. This is where our toolbox talks come in and information on operations procedure are exchanged between staff and management and upgraded with safety on the mind of all concerned. Free health insurance for physical and emotional wellbeing.

73) Q; What must be done on staff induction on (COSHH)?

Upon induction each employee is required to do a manual handling course and a control of substances-hazardous to health (COSHH) course. These courses are an invaluable source to the employee regarding injury prevention. We hope that the board of directors will continue to support us regarding the necessity of this course.

74) Q; How should organisation deals with First Aid?

A; Organisation should have a well stock and equipped room for any person requiring first aid and

several members of the work force are Qualified first aiders to cover each

department, the first aid box is checked every week and whenever is used healthy

competition

Must advertise on their notice boards about benefit of having healthier lifestyles and we receive further assistance from the local health centre, however, any support and advice from the board of Directors will be warmly accepted

75) Q; What include good physical working conditions?

A; These include lighting, ventilation, noise, space and equipment.

Lighting

The lighting is adequate for the operation that we are required to achieve and is regularly tested.

The ventilation system

The ventilation system is state of the art and works well all year round regardless of what of what our operations are.

Noise

Noise at times can be concern, however employee can obtained ear protection from stores along with any personal protection equipment that is required for any operation. All employees must wear safety glasses when entering workshops

Space and equipment. There must be plenty of

space the offices and in the workshop. Office equipment is ergonomically designed to reduce stress and fatigue. Workshop machinery is strategically place so the space in the workshop can be used with maximum effect

76)Q: What is the important of sanitation?

The cleaning of all areas is paramount and is done on daily basis. Emergency exit are kept clear of rubbish at all times, toilet washing and changing facilities are also cleaned on daily basis. A clean and bright atmosphere helps to maintain positive attitude in the workforce

There must be good and healthy report with employees regarding health issues in the work place and they understand the importance of being in good health.

77) Q; What are some health risks?

A; There are some Health Hazards in some of the operations for example cut and bruises, finger traps, crushed limbs, fumes inhalation, burns, Arc flashes from welding, trips and falls. These are few examples of some of the risk is an employee will face when working at some establishment

78)Q; What is AIDS ?

AIDS (Acquired Immune Deficiency Syndrome) is a disease caused by a latent slow- acting virus, the Human Immunodeficiency Virus (HIV) which destroys part of the body's immune system leaving it unable to defend itself against infectious viruses and certain cancers.

79)Q: How is Aids transmit?

AIDS is transmitted mainly in three ways, namely:

through unprotected anal, vaginal and possibly oral sex with an infected partner;

through intravenous drug users (particularly mainline drug users) sharing syringes and needles, and also through blood transfusions of infected blood, although this is extremely rare because of stringent testing; and

c. from an infected mother to her unborn child, i.e., placental transmission.

One cannot catch AIDS from:

sharing cups and eating utensils;

mosquitoes and insects;

towels;

hugging;

shaking hands;

giving blood ;

kissing;

swimming pools; and

toilet seats.

80)Q; Can Aids is Preventable

AIDS is preventable and the choice lies in the hands of each individual. If one sticks to one partner for a lifetime, there is usually no chance of contracting this disease unless one of the partners is unfaithful or contracts it through another means of transmission such as a blood transfusion

Q; What must organisation do regarding AID?

A; They must declared persons employed with any blood born viruses for example, Acquired Immune Deficiency Syndrome (AID) or Hepatitis B or C.

81) Q; How should cafeteria be kept?

A; The cafeteria is clean, well-lighted and peaceful atmosphere were an employee can relax, have lunch or quick refreshment break. It is staffed by four people, each of them work to very high food safety standards and high standard of cleanliness.

82) Q; Give an example of how organisation could conclude their report.

A; There had been no report of serious injury, only minor superficial injuries, for example cut and bruises during the last twelve months. There have been six recorded absentees with the yearly cold and flu and incident have decreased by 40% compare to the year before, I am pleased to inform the Board that 9% of our workforce is registered disable and all are performing satisfactorily. This report discuss the section mentioned thoroughly and as the board can see that the working environment in our company is safe place to work.

I hope that the Board of Directors is satisfied with our safety standard of work and if the Board has any recommendations we will implement it straight away. I will like to take the opportunity to thank board of directors for their support over the last twelve months.

83)Q; How do organisations deals with duty of care

A: The company must have a DUTY OF CARE towards staff, prisoners, contractors and visitors who have reason to be at the premises. This means Serco must provide a safe place of work, provide safe plant and equipment, safe systems of work and safe, competent fellow employees. The company must also have responsibility for the health, safety and welfare of all staff.

Health - Protecting the minds and bodies of people from illness concerning procedures or processes used in the workplace.

Safety - To protect people from physical injury

Welfare The provision of facilities to maintain the health and wellbeing of individuals at work place

84) Q; Write summary of safety management course

A; A work mission statement can be think safe and work safe"

Health - Protecting the minds and bodies of people from illness concerning procedures or processes used in the workplace.

Safety - To protect people from physical injury

Welfare; The provision of facilities to maintain the health and wellbeing of individuals at work place

All employers owes duty of care towards staff, contractors and visitors who have reason to be at the work place This means business must provide a safe place of work, provide safe plant and equipment, safe systems of work and safe, competent fellow employees. Employers also have responsibility for the health, safety and welfare of all staff and visitors

85)Q: where is Health and Safety important?

Health and safety is essential in all work places; in door, out door, day down or night, rainy or dry land, sea, in space or earth in fact in the universe. There is some specific safety requirement in certain work such as motor mechanic, plumbing electricity, and kitchen. The universe will not function without effective and efficient health and safety.

86)Q: what is the One of the most important to consider before start work?

The main points of this safety management course, an organization must consider more than several safety points before the commencement of any operations. A safe working environment is absolutely in today's businesses to meet the rule s of the health and safety at work act 1974.

A business must adopt ways in making the work place safe and free from any accidents as much as possible with the welfare of all concerned

It is very important for employee and employers to adhere to their responsibility. Management must support the implementation of safety programme, identify and prevent hazards, enforce safe behaviour; workers must be prepared, present the operation and test employee performance.

87) Q; summary employers responsibility

A; Protect others against Health and Safety risks from work activities.

Provide safe means of entry and exit. Provide a safe working environment. Provide safe plant and equipment. Provide safe systems of work.

88) Q; summary of employee responsibility

A: Take reasonable care of yourself and other. Co-operate with staff

Not interfere with, or misuse articles/equipment provided for health and safety purposes, such as Personal Protective Equipment (PPE), electrical equipment (TV, kettle fan), etc. Work in a safe manner (safe system of work)

Clean up spillages immediately they occur

Identify potential hazards and risks Report hazards to staff

Safe Systems of Work - How we work or expect to carry out our work in a safe manner (avoid taking short-cuts)

89)Q; What is Hazard -

A; A substance or process that has the potential to cause harm.

90) Q; summarise how to deal with electricity at work?

A; Workplaces must be orderlies with good ventilation, lighting, colour coding for safe identification, use of appropriate machine guards. Precaution of using electricity, ladders and all equipment must be used according to the manufacture recommendation or requirement

Principle Hazards include; electric shock Electric burns Arcing Portable electrical equipment Secondary hazards

Mains voltage; This is the common voltage in domestic premises and workplaces, normally taken from 3-pin socket points and usually supplied between 220v & 240v

92) **Q:** Explain Classes of Fire

Class A:

Solid materials; wood, paper,

cardboard, textiles, furniture

Fire extinguisher Water

Class B:

paints, oils, fats

Liquids/Liquefied solids;

Fire extinguisher Foam, Dry powder, Co2

Class C:

Natural gas, propane, butane.

Fire extinguisher Foam, dry powder

Class E:

Electrical

Fire extinguisher Co2

Class F:

Cooking oils

Fire extinguisher Wet chemical

Fire Hoses:

4 on each wing (2 x upper, Lower landings).

These are locked - Must be extended by at least 2m before system will activate.

93)**Q**; When must hose not to be used?

fire hoses are not to be used for cleaning showers.

Fire blankets: Wing servery area.

Water: At specific points throughout

the prison.

C02: As above.

Foam: As above.

94) **Q;** What is fire evacuation procedure

If there are burglar bars on the windows of a building, ensure there is an alternative easy route of escape from a building. Children should be wrapped in blankets to protect them against flames. If a large area is on fire, exit diagonally, upwind, in order to escape from the heated area more quickly. Never move upwind towards the centre of the fire and never downwind as that is where the heat is at its worst. Proceed to a predetermined location, such as a common or declared emergency shelter. Take the following steps:

a. Sound the alarm immediately.

b. Evacuate all people and pets from the building.

c. Close up inter-leading doors as you exit.

d. Disconnect the electric power before attempting to extinguish the fire.

e. Aim the extinguisher or water jet at the centre of the fire.

f. If the floor is burning, direct the jet from the bottom upwards.

g. Do not enter a burning room or building.

h. If someone is running with burning clothes on, catch and roll them in a blanket.

i. Do not pour water on burning liquids.

j. Use wet blankets to smother fires.

k. When someone is trapped in a burning car, do not break the window's unless you are sure the door can be opened. The influx of air will fan the flames.

l. When trapped in a burning building, cover your mouth with a wet handkerchief.

m. Be careful of poisonous gases.

n. Move along the sides of walls so that you do not lose your way.

o. Wet the roofs of other buildings in the vicinity to prevent fires from spreading.

p. Notify the fire officials as soon as possible, e.g. the local fire brigade.

q. Always check fire extinguishers regularly to ensure they are in good working order.

95) **Q;** summarise how to deal with Fire prevention at work?

A: Fire prevention and protection can be achieved by including workers in any prevention measures such as placing fire extinguishers in strategic places in the premises. The induction must include training for the use of fire extinguishers. In case of fire, exclude one or two of the elements, such as oxygen, heart, fuel. Workers must be diligent when using electricity, chemical, heated surfaces cigarettes sparks.

All employees and employers must know the use of all type of fire extinguishers, classification of fire, prevention and orderly evacuation in case of fire.

Another method is to introduce some rules such as no smoking in the areas containing flammable liquid.

The prevention can also achieved by the regular maintained of all electrical

96)**Q;** Explain personal protective equipment

A: Examples of PPE in use at workshop - Eye protection, hand protection, (work and clinical gloves), safety footwear, HV clothing, filter masks.

All equipment, including clothing for protection against the weather, intended to be worn or held by a person at work, which protects them against risks to their health and safety.

PPE is not ordinary working clothes, uniforms and protective equipment worn in sports competitions/pastimes.

PPE should only be used as a last resort i.e. when all other options have been exhausted where by not putting people in a risk situation.

97) **Q;** what happen if employee refused to use PPE.

A; Refusal / failure of person(s) to wear PPE when it is identified through risk assessment that it is necessary will lead to disciplinary action against that person(s)

98)**Q:** What type of PPE and management responsibility on it.

Personal protection equipment (PPE) and clothing must be fire retardant and provided to and member of the employee that requires them. There is a range of personnel protection equipment and the basics include hard hats, safety grasses, thick groves, and overall and safety boots. Depending on the circumstances, there is PPE to protect the worker and there must be no excuse not to use them. Most personnel protection equipment is easy to use; however training must be given for the use of all PPE

The management of safety programmed s is an essential part of any business and hence to make sure that employee that in order to do their work right without incident by using them the correct way. Also the supervisor must make sure that the employee has correct knowledge of how they must protect themselves which can be possible by supplying safety courses, for example;

99)**Q**; What must organisation do in major emergency

A; If there is major emergency, the Civil Defence procedure will take over to protect property and life; for example a disaster of large fire, mine collapse or floods. Emergencies services are there to help rescue and recover trapped persons, to help the injuries and to protect the properties from destruction if possible.

Civil defence

The aim and objective of CCS must be fully implemented when needed Civil Defence in Peacetime Act 1986 chapter 22 states "The Act is to enable local authorities to use their civil defence resources in connection with emergencies and disasters unconnected with any hostile attract by a foreign power (26th June 1986)"The Act also authorise local authorities to provide any services maintained by them and to provide relief and help were possible for the protection life properties and the environment.

The aim and objective of the (CCS) civil Contingencies secretariat must be call to place example civil defence Act 1948 section 2 and section 4A give the responsibilities of the local authorities. It also covers emergencies of both men made and natural disaster

Staff must be aware of how to deal with and cope with any type of disaster\emergency example procedure to deal with firepower failure, refuse removal, hurricanes, earthquakes, floods ECT. Must know when and when not to use protective equipment and clothing

100) **Q:** why is it important to have first aid at work?

A: In any business, there must be provision for at least basic first aid from cleaning and covering of injury to perform chest compression on a patient whose heart has stopped. This first aid action may prevent someone losing any limbs or making full recoveries from a heart attack. Little things such as cleaning diet from some one's eye could prevent blankness in that eye. Therefore, basic safety rules are also important.

101) **Q;** why should organisation have basic rules.

Basic safety rules are mandatory such as wearing of ear defenders, hard hat, safety grass, safety boots in a specific area must be obeyed to prevent injuries all employee must be informed with some safety rules by either signage, such as no entry.no smoking or naked lights. these rules are developed to protect workers from injury and anyone who interferes with or purposely damage safety equipment should be prosecuted.

102) **Q;** What is the likelihood that harm may occur?

A; Other things that affect workers include; lack of knowledge or skill, altitude of employee, physical unsuitability, physical or improper mechanical are some the means that can be identified as unsafe.

reduce the risk of injury

do check trolley before using. do not tie off brakes these are a safety feature.

Check doors are secure and will not open when moving. DO NOT ride on them.

Operating is easy, squeeze brake and push DO NOT run.

DO NOT race or cut corners; keep a safe distance between you and other trolley pushers.

Wear suitable/sensible clothing and footwear NO FLIP FLOPS Reduce the load. Share your load Know your own personal capability.

Risk Assessment - A process used to decide on priorities and to set objectives for eliminating hazards and reducing risks.

Reduce risk

Accident - Is any unplanned event that results in ill health to people, damage or loss to property, plant, materials or the environment.

Near miss - Any incident that could result in an accident.

103) **Q;** Explain RIDDOR

A; Dangerous Occurrence - A near miss which could lead to serious injury or loss of life-reportable to the Health and Safety Executive (HSE) under Reporting of injuries, Diseases and Dangerous Occurrences (RIDDOR) Regulations.

104) **Q;** Explain COSHH
(control of substances hazardous to health)

COSHH covers most substances hazardous to health found in the workplace.

105) **Q;** What does COSHH include?
A; Any substance used directly in work activities e.g. solvents, paints, adhesives and cleaning materials.

Substances generated during work processes or activities e.g. dust from sanding and fumes from welding.

Naturally occurring substances e.g. grain dust.

Do not empty COSHH items into another bottle or containers that state it is something else it is dangerous

106) Q; Give summary of some manual handling

A:

a. Lifting a load which is too heavy or cumbersome - may result in back injury. Poor posture or lifting techniques may result in back injury.

b. Dropping a load may result in foot injury.

c. Lifting sharp, edged or hot things may result in hand injuries

107) **Q;** Give summary of how to lift load safely?

a. Lift smoothly to knee level then waist level. No further bending of the back.

b. Ensure clear visibility - move forward without twisting. Keep load close to waist. Turn by moving feet. Keep head up do not look at load.

c. Set load down at waist level then knee then to the floor keeping your back straight at all times.

108) **Q;** Who need to be trained first in organisation.

Supervisors must be trained properly before allowing to train others.

Implement fully the aim of loss control to prevent or reduce accident considering the three phases;

prevention of injuries, control damage and loss control.

All workers must co-operate with the supervisors to implement a corrective interview adopted by the company to correcting unsafe acts.

109) **Q;** summarise how you will be able to utilise these theories when working in every day situation.

A; The theories that I gave learnt speak for itself, considering the summarise above supported by some figure demonstration. The feedback from my tutor on all the eight units of the course demonstrate invaluable information that I have assimilated on safety management; work place, good housekeeping, fire prevention and procedure, protection, protective equipment, clothing management of safety programmes, civil emergency procedure, civil defence, legislation, first aid basic safety rules.

With these theories gain, I am confidence to put them into practice to protect myself and other employees as well as the business that i may be request to advice on safety management. I can impact my knowledge to others welfare and well-being and can demonstrate safety work including; reduction of risk of injury\assessment of risk. And most hazards include the main voltage, employers and employee responsibilities. Working as a freelance, I am optimism to provide very good report and recommendation and requirement by quoting the health and safety laws to back up my knowledge. Including (COSHH) control of substances hazardous to health, (RIDDOR) Reporting of injuries, Diseases and Dangerous Occurrences Regulations, manual handling. With the aim to reduce risk, accident, near miss. With health and safety rules, there is no room for compromise as the law requirement must be adhere to always. I am confidence not only to prevent accidents\injury but to deal with any emergencies include natural or manmade. I can offer relishing course to the work force to update them of any addition rules and also provide induction to new employees.

These theories will help me and others such as my family to be safe at home as well as outdoor and indoor activities. Such as athletics, football and many sporting event

In fact I am confidence to apply for a job as Health and Safety Executive (HSE) which is something I will enjoy doing.

In conclusion the course has benefited me to be safe at work at all time

Control of Substances Hazardous to Health COSHH

COSHH covers most substances hazardous to health found in the workplace.

110) **Q**; How do some employee become more risk due to extra income

A; Higher Earnings

Some employees want to earn more money, and to prove themselves worthy of promotion and higher earnings. It is here that these employees take chances to increase their output just to impress their seniors. They could endanger their lives in this attempt.

111) **Q;** How do some employee become more risk due Security of their job

A; Some employees may endanger their lives just to retain their jobs, particularly in an economic depression when jobs are not freely available. Physical safety measures could be ignored if the employee becomes desperate not to lose his job. Supervisors must change the employee's ideas of how job security can best be achieved. They must make it clear that job security and economic security are inextricably linked and that it is only by safe working habits that job retention./ security can be achieved.

112) **Q**; How do some employee become more risk due to Seeking approval of others

A: New employees could want to seek the approval of their peers. They may perform an unsafe act in the workplace to gain such approval. In most situations, employees will probably see greater advantage in doing the job the way their work group does, even at the risk of displeasing the supervisor and endangering their own lives. The desire for acceptance becomes a risky venture if unsafe acts are among the work habits sanctioned by the group because new employees may absorb these habits in order to be accepted by the group.

113) **Q**: How do some employee become more risk due to extra income Difficulties in Inattention

A; Sometimes an employee manifests temporary inattentive behaviour. Some of the causes could be as follows:

1. Temporary Periods of Stress

Whatever their ages, employees are subject to temporary periods of unusual stress. If accidents are to be prevented in such periods of tension, it is necessary to assist employees to cope with their times of travail, at least to the extent of providing safeguards and helping with solutions which are within the supervisor's control.

1. Effect of Personal Problem

Inattention could in many instances be attributed to personal difficulties such as domestic

circumstances which cannot be shed by employees as they daily enter the workplace. It could be helpful if the supervisor became a good listener during these periods, although it is

undesirable for the supervisor to become intimately involved with the personal life of the employee. If an employee is enabled to talk out a problem with a sympathetic and understanding listener, he or she could see it in a different and more constructive light.

114) Q; What is the effect of Job-related Conditions on employee?

Sometimes a number of accident ingredients are present

which are beyond the control of the employee. These pre-existing conditions could be hazardous. The employees maybe unaware of these hazards, and their reaction to the situation, if they become aware, may be trial-and-error. If their response does not work, emotions may be aroused. The momentarily blind act or emotional act is often an unsafe act.

The continuance of adverse job conditions can have an ominous and frustrating influence on employee conduct. This frustration may manifest itself in aggression, rigidity and childishness.

115) **Q;** How can frustration in an employee be noticed?

A: These frustrations could also manifest

themselves through unsafe acts.

Distractions related to Work-place Location and Job Monotony

Work-place locations can lead to unsafe acts if they subject the employee to competing demands, e.g., where workstations are near the toilets or a cafeteria. Monotony can also be troublesome as it often results in self-induced distractions. Supervisors should be on the lookout for any form of distraction.

116) **Q;** What is one way to alleviate employee problems?

Communication is the Key to Inattention

The supervisor should communicate meaningfully with the employee. Sometimes the source of frustration can be rectified by the supervisor. The supervisor must try to pinpoint the problem clearly. Sometimes the difficulty may have to be resolved jointly by the supervisor and the subordinate. At other times, the problem must be resolved unilaterally by either the employee or the supervisor.

117) **Q;** How can employee be affected by Perceptual Difficulties

A; It could occur that the reason for an unsafe act emanates from instantaneous perceptual failure. The worker has been bombarded with too much information at one time. There are too many signals reaching the worker and causing a wrong response or a late response; because of a lack of perception, the worker can react in an uninformed or emotional manner; the worker could also react to a compelling signal without awareness of counter-indications. These kinds of difficulties are present in many industrial jobs. Workers have to adjust to the safe sequencing of their work, and this takes time. There may be blinding hazards of which the worker is unaware. Supervisors should ensure that the perceptual requirements of a job are not unreasonable. All jobs should in the beginning take account of the perceptual limitations of human beings. As part of job training, supervisors should emphasise the perceptual aspects of a job, and make the safety requirements for a job as clear as possible so that the employee's perceptions are realistically specific to the situation and not based on wants and prior experience alone. The supervisor must make sure that the employee can pick up all the signs of a job in time and that the employee can make the correct response and choice to the signs when counter-indications occur. The right sequence of responses must be responded to when demands are concurrent, but not contradictory. For this purpose, lecturing (counselling) is insufficient; there must also be practical coaching. Employees must also be protected against errant performance during the training period so that they are not injured by unsafe acts.

118) **Q;** What is the role and functions of the manager in the prevention of accidents.

It is the function of the manager to monitor and prevent accidents. Management has the best opportunity and ability to initiate the prevention of accidents, and therefore it should assume responsibility for any occurrences. Every accident occurring in a manager's department is a reflection on his ability to manage. He is obliged to supply a safe environment and tools, and safe methods of working. Morally, the manager is bound to maximise a company's profits, and minimise the losses and see to it that the company remains in business. If people are continually injured on duty, no one will be willing to work for such a company.

119) **Q;** Functions of the Supervisor in the prevention of accidents.

The supervisor has a significant role to play in accident prevention because he controls the work performance of the subordinates and can contribute considerably toward accident prevention. The supervisor or foreman is a keyperson because he is directly involved in and responsible for the day- to-day activities of the plant or factory or business venture. The supervisor should know the standard methods of safe working and should be able to communicate in such a manner that upper and lower echelons understand him clearly. However, it should be stated at the outset that supervisors are not expected to become safety engineers - they cannot be expected to build machine guards, design the danger out of machinery, determine the noxious qualities of materials, establish weight loads or other operational limitations for equipment used in the lifting or moving of materials, or design safety equipment and protective clothing for operators. Supervisors need not be experts in zoning, layout or colour coding of the factory. Supervisors are concerned with the application of materials and the effect of machinery on the employee. They must see to it that the workers are properly trained in the use of the machinery or equipment, in the safe execution of whatever processes and operations their jobs require, and in safe activity and movement within the work area. They must reinforce good working habits which represent the safest as well as the most efficient and effective method of production.

Supervisors must be competent motivators of people. They must motivate people to practise safety in the workplace. In order to motivate and correct others, the supervisors themselves must be motivated and adequately trained for the job at hand. It must be borne in mind that safety is trainable - safe acts and unsafe acts are learnt and can be taught. New employees must not leant safe or unsafe acts by experience. This could maim or kill them.

Safety is also controllable. Most accidents result from the unsafe acts of employees rather than from uncontrollable physical conditions. Even when physical conditions are hazardous, accidents occur usually because of the acts of employees within the dangerous environment. Supervisors must not attribute accidents to carelessness because it is then difficult to find a cure for such a broad classification of causes of accidents. The supervisor should go much deeper into the matter by trying to ascertain what the cause of the carelessness or thoughtlessness was. The cause is usually found in the drives underlying human behaviour and other factors forming part of human nature and which affect safe job performance.

120) **Q;** Why should the supervisor be held responsible for accident prevention?

A; The supervisor has to assume responsibility for accident prevention for the following reasons:

Accidents are usually preventable, but once an accident has occurred, the severity of the injury cannot be reversed.

The supervisor is responsible for good housekeeping and a safe environment.

The maximum quantity and quality of goods and services must be produced at the lowest cost with the least disruption. If and when an accident occurs, it could cause delays, damaged material, damaged equipment, dissatisfied customers, and a repetition, or duplication of the same work.

The supervisor is usually in direct contact with the subordinates (workers) and is therefore in the best position to know their weaknesses and strengths.

The supervisor must prevent buck-passing, and wrong mental altitudes

121) **Q:** steps be taken in safety training

A: The supervisor must determine and define what has to be learnt, and what knowledge and skills must be acquired by the old and new employee. The supervisor must look at three kinds of hazards in the workplace, viz., machine hazards, work-place hazards and employee acts (safe and unsafe). After the supervisor has decided what is to be learnt, he must then arrange to create an environment which is conducive to learning. A supervisor must not assume that:

a. An employee has understood the meaning of words used,

b. The employee is listening,

c. The employee is learning and will remember, and

d. The entire subject has been covered by himself.

122) Q: How should supervisor communicate with employee?

The supervisor must ensure that his communication to subordinates is effective, i.e., he must see that there are no distractions while he is instructing the worker; he must find out how much the worker already knows; he must use simple vocabulary; he must organise his presentations properly and logically; he must check periodically to see that employees are listening and understanding; he must use repetition; and he must provide for follow-up. It is essential that the supervisor has an interest in his subordinates and does not merely treat them as factors of production. This attitude will ensure a good rapport between supervisor and subordinates.

122) **Q** What must the manager or supervisor do to make sure the employee have absorbed lectures?

Employees will not merely learn safe acts by listening to lecturers; there has to be practise as well.

The following steps must be taken after each lecture-session:

a. Enough supervised practice must be permitted in each job task to assure that the trainees have genuinely learnt the right and safe method.

b. The job should be broken down into training tasks in order, not to put too heavy a learning burden on the employees.

c. Rest periods should be provided at frequent intervals to offset fatigue.

d. What is learnt in theory must be able to be put in to practice; in other words, learning must be realistic and feasible. The main task of the supervisor is there to coach subordinates.

The following methods of coaching can be used:

a. The job method must be explained to indicate why the job is done in a particular manner to enhance safety,

b. The demonstration method can be used in coaching,

c. Practice cuing and feedback can be used,

d. Safe performance should be rewarded by showing approval, and

e. Unsafe acts should be detected and immediately corrected.

Such reinforcement often serves as motivation enough for the employee's continuation of safe job performance.

107 Q; What is the role of supervisor in preventing future accidents.

A: He must:

1. Identify the dysfunctional situation,

2. Understand the reason(s) for the existence of the dysfunction(s),

3. Select an appropriate remedy for the situation,

4. Apply the remedy, and

5. Follow up.

123) **Q;** what is the meaning of loss pf control

A; Control means to guide something in the direction it is intended to go. To control means seeing that everything occurs in conformity with established rules and expressed commands. Control involves determining where you want to go, observing to see that you keep on the course and schedule, and giving orders when necessary to correct variances.

124) **Q:** What is the definition loss control

A; Loss control is the elimination of all errors, incidents, and undesired or unwanted events caused by improper planning, organising, leading and controlling which result in business losses and which can be obviated by using sound management principles and practices.

125) **Q;** How many phases to lose control?

A: There are three phases to loss control, namely, the prevention of injuries; the control of damage; and lastly, loss control. Loss control must prevent not only injury, but also prevent damage to property and fire losses. Loss control must thwart the interruption of the normal course of business.

126) **Q;** What is the main aim of loss of control?

The prime aim of loss control is to prevent accidents from occurring, i.e., to prevent downgrading incidents. Accidents are unplanned and uncontrolled events which can be caused by unsafe acts and/or unsafe conditions. All unsafe acts must be eliminated as far as possible. Unsafe conditions are caused by any departure from accepted safety standards.

To prevent or reduce accidents, unsafe acts and unsafe conditions must be reduced to the absolute minimum.

127) **Q;** What is the consequence of unsafe act and condition at workplace?

A: If unsafe acts and unsafe conditions are not kept to an absolute minimum, it could lead to many man-days being lost in the factory and ultimately the whole country. Besides the money being paid out by the Employers liability insurance, there are also several "hidden costs" which must be borne by the employer. For example, there is time lost through injury to the worker; there is time lost by other workers who stop work out of curiosity, sympathy or a desire to assist the injured person; there is time lost by the foreman, supervisors and other staff members who have to assist the injured person; there could also be damage to machinery and tools; and the production process could be disrupted thus failing to meet orders on time.

128) **Q;** What is the term "Creative" in health and safety?

A: There are many forms and method of correcting unsafe acts it is straight pointy. Creative is the time when the supervisor/interviewer must be all ears. He must try to establish what went wrong and what the causes of the unsafe acts have been. The interviewer must not make premature judgements of causes and must not force these judgements on the employee.

129) **Q;** How can supervisor find out the cause of accident.

A; In order to get at the genuine causes, the supervisor must find out how the employees view the accident. Such a step. It requires the supervisor to withhold blame or criticism and to invite the employee to talk. There must be a permissive atmosphere and a sincere effort in listening to what the employee has to say.

During the corrective interview, the supervisor must assist the employee to accept new and better methods of doing a job without the risk of injury. It is also possible to ascertain during a corrective

interview whether the unsafe act was caused by temporary factors such as stress, or whether it had become an established manner of doing things. The unsafe act could have been due to perceptual

130) **Q;** what is the next step when the cause established?

A; Once the cause of an unsafe act is ascertained and common understanding reached on it, a further agreement is needed - an agreement concerning the mode of correction. Supervisors should always try to make subordinates understand the wisdom of a solution to a problem. Once the solution has been agreed upon, there must be close follow-up and monitoring to ensure that the worker is performing the work in the prescribed manner and that good habits are being cultivated and reinforced.

131) **Q;** Is it possible to fail to establish the Couse of accident through corrective interview?

A; Yes, It failure, - this too can be established during the corrective interview.

Because the corrective interview is conducted in an atmosphere of permissiveness, it does not mean that there is no room for firmness.

132) **Q**; what must employer do if the suspected employee is unhelpful?

A; At times, firm and even drastic measures are required. As a last resort, in order to protect both the employee and the fellow workers from the employee's wilfully dangerous acts, the use of disciplinary action may be justified. When supervisors try to remedy unsafe acts, their firmness is not therefore discarded, but should be brought into play at the appropriate times.

133) **Q**; Can employee unsafe behaviour be changed?

A; It must be remembered that unsafe behaviour can be modified to bring about safe behaviour. Of course, all this depends on the willingness of the subordinates to be taught. One can take a horse to the water, but one cannot make it drink.

134) **Q;** Name few causes of incidents

There are four basic causes of accidents, namely, unsafe conditions; lack of knowledge and/or skill; physical or mental defects; and improper attitudes.

135) **Q;** In business, how is incident downgraded?

There are four major elements in the business concern which contribute to downgrading incidents or causes accidents namely people, equipment, material and environment

136) **Q;** Briefly describe People cause or downgrade accidents.

A; The human element is directly involved with most accidents, since what he does or fails to do is seen as the immediate causal factor.

137) **Q:** Briefly describe equipment as cause or downgrade accidents.

A: Tools and machinery are a big target for mechanical safeguarding and operator training. The improper design of controls and displays on machinery and equipment have been frequently named as' the source or cause of many downgrading incidents involved with safety, quality and production problems.

138) **Q:** Briefly describe material people as cause or downgrade accidents.

A; The material people use is another major source of incident cause. These elements are a source of serious injury for a staggering number of people. Material can be sharp, heavy, hot, or toxic.

139) **Q;** Briefly describe environment as cause or downgrade accidents.

A; The work environment is a cause of a number of diseases and health-related conditions. The environment is also a major source of incident causes associated with absenteeism and poor work quality.

140) **Q;** What are remedies of accidents

A; There are four remedies to accidents, namely, engineering revision; education, training, persuasion and appeal; proper personnel placement and adjustment; and discipline.

141) **Q:** Who is responsibility for accident prevention

There are two parties responsible for accident prevention, namely, the employer who is responsible for safe working conditions and the worker who is responsible for safe work, i.e., the worker must develop safe working habits and use safeguards and protective equipment properly.

An accident prevention programme needs the unqualified support of management who also have to vole/authorise the necessary funds for the accident prevention programme. Accident prevention methods in most large companies have become part of the normal managerial function because a low accident rate saves money for the company.

142) **Q:** What are the cost of accidents.

A: There are, in fact, several types of costs involved when the frequency of accidents is high. Accidents always have financial or other implications which are usually more severe than anticipated.

143) **Q;** What is the Cost to the Victim

A; The employee's capital asset is invested in his ability to attend and perform at this place of work. Take away that from him, and his losses begin to accumulate quickly. His costs are very personal ones, and because he is at the sharp end of the incident, he will naturally feel his position strongly. The victim's costs are by no means exclusively financial. These might well include:

Pain and suffering.

Loss of wages.

Loss of overtime.

Loss of promotional prospects.

Curtailment of leisure activities.

Long-term disablement.

Loss of social interaction.

Psychological damage.

Family stress.

Perhaps even death..

144) **Q;** What is the Cost to the Company in accident?.

The company will suffer a different range of costs:.

Lost production.

Damage to equipment.

Repair and replacement cost.

Consequential overtime costs.

Increased insurance premiums.

Legal penalties.

Cost of investigation and documentation.

Compensation expenses.

Industrial relations problems.

Loss of goodwill and reputation.

As mentioned, there are also a variety of "hidden costs", which the company does not need and cannot really afford. No employer can afford to ignore the cost of accidents and injuries. To take a lax view of a poor safety record is just plain bad management.

145) **Q;** What is the Cost of accident to the Nation

A; A company may be seen as a microcosm of the nation when considering cost. The nation will therefore suffer the accrued expense of production losses associated with injury and accidents.

146) **Q**; What is the cost to the company Manager

The manager is right in the front line of the battle to cut costs; it is part of his job to operate his department efficiently and economically. Accidents represent failure and wastage and are in the main preventable. Therefore it is the duty of every manager to try and contain or prevent accidents whenever and wherever possible.

147) **Q;** How can loss control be enhanced?

A; Loss control can be enhanced through periodic safety inspections which take the following forms: Safety Audit.

Safety Survey, Safety Tour

Safety Sampling, Scheduled Safety Inspection, controlling losses by teaching people, Readiness, Association.Application

148) **Q;** Briefly describe Safety Audit as loss of control remedy

A; This is weekly or periodically carry out inspection of all resources and draw up remedies to prevent accident

149) **Q:** Briefly describe Safety survey as loss of control remedy

A: This is a more sharply focussed examination, a hard look at an area which has a known problem.

150) **Q**: Briefly describe Safety tour as loss of control remedy.

A; This is merely an unscheduled inspection of a work area to cheek on such aspects as good housekeeping.

151) **Q;** Briefly describe Safety sampling as loss of control remedy

A: This is a procedure in which a team of trained observers carries out a regular tour of the work area, armed with pad and pencil.

152) **Q:** Briefly describe Scheduled Safety Inspection as loss of control remedy

A: This is the routine, disciplined, solid, no-nonsense technique which turns over the stones to reveal the unsafe acts and conditions lurking beneath.

Inspections and checking are an integral part of loss control and loss prevention. The whole idea is to cast a critical eye over the workplace, its hardware, its working methods, its general condition, i.e., to discover hazards before they harm the unwary employee.

153) **Q:** Briefly describe controlling losses by teaching people as means of loss of control remedy.

A; It is almost certain that losses will be out of control if the workers lack the necessary knowledge, motivation, ability and skill to do their jobs properly and know how to prevent accidents. It is the duty of every manager and supervisor to develop people to their fullest potential to prevent incidents from occurring. Losses are more likely to be under control when employees are informed and interested and skilful in their jobs. This process of development brings about numerous benefits to the business, e.g., increased productivity, reduced labour turnover, better employee morale and fewer accidents, to name but a few benefits of training and development.

For an employee to leant new skills and to becoming knowledgeable about his work environment and his functions, he must display the following attributes.

154) **Q;** Briefly describe Readiness as means to loss of control remedy

A: Employees will learn best when they are willing and ready to learn.

The more a response leads To effects that are motivationally satisfying, the more likely it is to be learned and repeated. For the best results in a teaching/leaming situation, one should always accentuate the positive, i.e., through praise and reward.

155) **Q;** Briefly describe Association as means to loss of control remedy

A: Learning something new is made easier if the learning can be built upon something one already knows. In training or teaching, it is best to proceed from the known to the unknown or new, to start with simple steps and gradually build up to the new and more difficult tasks or ideas.

156) **Q:** Briefly describe Application as means to loss of control remedy

A; The more an idea or task is applied, the better it is understood and remembered, it is essential that learning is achieved by doing the work.

157) **Q**; What is the seriousness of losses and the necessity for loss control.

A: Every incident or accident costs the company or the individuals either money or some or other personal loss. There could even be damage to machinery and equipment. The factory could also be destroyed by fire or explosion. It is essential, therefore, to teach people how to reduce accidents as far as possible to safeguard their own lives and business property, and to ensure that they can continue working without disruption, or obviate being retrenched because of a shut-down or for other reasons

158) **Q;** who is responsible to alert health risk?

A: It is the function of the human resources manager to be alert to these health risks and to try and prevent them before they take root and become chronic or serious illnesses. It is necessary to ensure that the workplace is such that occupational health is promoted and that health programmes are introduced to reduce health and safety risks to the absolute minimum

159) **Q;** what equipment must organisation health care have to provide total health care for employee

If employers are serious about the health of their workers, they could have a total health care approach. This means that they could have the following machines on-site, i.e., an audiometer (an instrument to test hearing); an e.g. machine (to check heart functions); a vision screener to test sight; hearing protectors (ear-plugs and ear-muffs); a spirometer (an instrument for measuring lung capacity); a digital blood pressure meter, and any other health records to be kept on the computer.

160) **Q:** Name some health risk which can be found at workplace?

A: Some of the health risks which are found in the workplace and the substances which cause them, are listed below:

a. Arsenic - lung cancer and lymphoma;

b. Asbestos - white lung diseases, asbestosis, lung cancer, and cancer of other organs;

c. Benzene - leukaemia and aplastic anaemia;

d. - lung cancer;

e. Coke-oven waste - lung cancer and kidney cancer;

f. Cotton dust - brown lung diseases, chronic bronchitis and emphysema;

g. Lead - kidney diseases, anaemia and damage to the central nervous system, sterility, birth defects;

h. Radiation - cancer of the thyroid gland, lungs and legs, and leukaemia;

i. Carbon waste - black lung disease; and

j. Benzol chloride - brain cancer and cancer of the liver.

161) **Q**: Give an example of Colour Coding for Safety Identification in a factory?

A: It is usual practice in the factory set-up to colour code some hazardous areas, machinery or dangerous substances, e.g., the colour RED usually indicates danger; fire protection equipment or stop buttons and emergency stop controls; YELLOW usually indicates caution; and warnings of hazards from radio-activity; GREEN indicates the location of first aid facilities; location of gas masks; exit signs other than emergency; safety instruction signs; safe areas; parking areas; equipment storage; toilets; offices and entrances; light ORANGE is used on the inside surfaces of machine guards as well as the dangerous parts of a machine capable of cutting, shearing or crushing; the surfaces of protruding shafts, the faces of gear wheels and any rotating part of a machine. The intention is to draw immediate attention to any potential hazard.

162) **Q:** Why is it important to have proper factory Layout.

A; It is essential that the factory layout and premises in general are maintained in a good condition. This will minimise the risk of accidents.

163) **Q;** Name few things to improve factory layout?

A: Faulty design or maintenance of premises, obstruction of access routes and traffic aisles should be prevented. Floors should not be overcrowded/overloaded. Floor and wall openings, staircase wells, passenger and goods lift cages, gangways and overhead platforms should all be suitably fenced. Guard rails should be of adequate dimensions and strength, and toe- boards should be fitted on gangways passing over areas where people are working and where there is a danger of falling objects.

Suitable means of access to machinery and equipment should be provided so that maintenance teams are not required to perform dangerous or acrobatic manoeuvres in their regular work. Crush, nip or shear points between moving and stationary objects should be eliminated or guarded.

Emergency exits to ensure a means of escape in the event of fire should be sufficient in number, correctly positioned and signposted, and free from encumbrance. Good lighting is essential for the safe movement of persons, plant and equipment. Inadequate lighting levels may conceal obstacles or danger zones, whereas badly positioned or excessively powerful light sources may cause glare.

164) **Q**; What are the rules in handling of Ladders?

A:

a. There are a number of rules which have to be adhered to whilst handling/ using a ladder:

b. Avoid bringing a metal ladder near electricity (electrical overhead wires).

c. Place the ladder so that its feet are a quarter of its own length from the object it is resting against.

d. Let someone hold the ladder if it is not tied at the top.

e. Let the ladder extend for a considerable distance above its support in case it slips down.

Inspect ladders regularly to repair or replace defective rungs and other parts.

f. Rather varnish than paint a ladder because defects may be concealed by paint.

g. Keep ladders clean to expose defects.

h. Do not expose ladders to inclement weather.

i. Do not use ladders as scaffolding.

j. Haul tools and equipment up by rope instead of hanging them onto the sides or rungs of the ladder.

k. Do not leave a ladder where it may fall and be damaged.

l. Do not place ladders in front of doors which are regularly used as thoroughfares. The door could suddenly be opened, and you could be flung to the ground.

m. Equip the ladder with safety feet or non-skid devices.

n. Use both hands when climbing a ladder.

o. Only one person at a time should climb a ladder.

165) **Q:** What precaution must be taken concerning electricity?

A:To ensure a safe and uninterrupted supply of electricity, an industrialist must ensure that the electrical installations are correctly designed; proper and suitable equipment must be used; electrical installations and equipment must be maintained in accordance with planned maintenance programmes. A well-thought out planned maintenance programme of the electrical installation will ensure that regular cleaning, inspections, adjustment, testing and planned part replacement, arc carried out which, experience has shown, significantly reduces breakdowns, including dangerous breakdowns or dangerous conditions.

Personnel should only be permitted to work on electrical systems if the circuits have been isolated, i.e., switched off or if a lockout system has been secured. Electrocutions are frequently caused when personnel work on electrical equipment which they either believe or assume has been isolated.

There should also be electrical protective devices such as overload and fault protection mechanisms,

e.g. double insulated portable electric tools; double wound transformers; and earth-leakage systems, as described above. However, sometimes fault protection devices do network - this could lead to fires in storerooms and warehouses. The recommended protection of the electrical installation in storerooms or other areas where flammable materials are stored or used, is to provide earth-leakage devices on all circuits, which will either isolate the circuits or sound an alarm if a pre-set leakage current is exceeded.

166) **Q;** What precaution to be made on Company Vehicles

A: Company vehicles should be checked regularly for faulty brakes; faulty headlights; damaged connecting cables; general lighting; worn tyres; faulty windscreen wipers; defective steering wheels; broken windows; broken hooters; rear-view mirrors; engine idling; instruments; exhaust system; cooling system; and emergency equipment such as fire extinguishers, spare bulbs and emergency triangles.

167) **Q:** Describe some machines that need guard.

A; Machines that should be guarded may have one or more

of the following mechanisms:

- Rotating mechanisms
- In-running nip points
- Forming or bending mechanisms
- Cutting or shearing mechanisms
- Screw or worm mechanisms

168) **Q;** What equipment in machine mechanism might cause hazard?

A: A piece of equipment may use more than one basic mechanism and therefore present more than one type of hazardous exposure. A belt and pulley, for example, has a hazardous rotating mechanism and as well as hazardous in-running nip points. Circular saws, for instance, present the following hazards:

a. the natural characteristics of the wood which could make it dangerous, e.g., knots,

b. contact between a part of the worker's body and the saw teeth,

c. kickback of the stock (this is a particular characteristic of a circular ripping saw),

d. contact between a part of the worker's body and the saw transmission,

e. hands being drawn into the automatic feed device,

f. inadequacy of the machine guards, e.g., if the guard is incorrectly adjusted,

g. bad working practices, e.g., loose clothing getting entwined in the mechanisms,

h. noise, and

i. the stock being sawn.

169) Q; What is machine guard?

A; A machine guard is a barrier which suitably encloses the moving parts of a machine. It must prevent any part of the body from reaching under, over, around or through the guard and entering the danger zone.

170) **Q:** Why should machines be safeguarded?

A; It is necessary to safeguard machines because the injuries caused by machines could be severe, disabling and permanent; such injuries are generally preventable; danger can often be reduced or removed by mechanical safeguards; and workers realise that unguarded machinery is dangerous. The employer should spend money on the safeguarding of machinery to show his sincerity in protecting the workers from injury.

171) **Q**: What materials is used for machine guards?

A: The preferred material for guards, under most circumstances, is metal. The framework of guards is usually made from structural shapes such as pipe, strapping and bar or rod stock. Filler material generally is expanded metal, perforated metal, solid steel metal, or heavy wire mesh. Where visibility is required, guards of formed transparent plastic or of safety glass are widely used. An important factor in the design of a guard is to provide complete protection; the openings must be large enough to admit stock, but small enough to prevent a person or object from getting into the danger zone.

172) **Q**: Name some types of machine guards.

A: There are two classes of machine guards, namely, transmission guards and point of operation guards. There are three types of guards, namely:

1. Fixed Guards - these do not move with each operation,

2. Interlocking Guards - these guards prevent the controls of the machine from being used until the guard is moved into place, and

3. Automatic Guards - these prevent the machine operator from coming into contact with the dangerous parts of a machine while it is moving.

173) **Q:** What is requirements of machine guards?

A: Machine guards should comply with the following requirements:

a. They should afford the maximum protection possible,

b. The danger zone(s) should be blocked out during operation,

c. The guards should be corrosion-free and fire-resistant,

d. The guards should not produce splinters or pinch the operators,

e. The guards should be fixtures of the machinery,

f. The guards should not affect the efficiency of the machine, and

g. They should be strong enough to withstand normal wear and tear.

174) **Q;** How do machine guards help?

A: There are various machines in all type of business that can range from steel cutting to pumping concrete. Machine guilds are on one particular machine for a particular reason, for example, A

Gloucestershire Laith has a revolving head called "chuck". To use the chuck you must have a chuck key. The Lathe has a guard that is pulled over the chuck before the machine will start, if the key is left in the chuck, The Lathe cannot start as it preventing the guard being pull over it. The operator must remove the key to prevent the key from doing any damage.

175) **Q;** How does Angle grinder works?

A; Another example is the guard on an angle grinder which only lets a certain amount, of the grinding\cutting disc shown as a kickback is likely to happen when the disc has contacted the material being used to cut\gourd away. Machine guard is in place to prevent anything from being grabbed. Or falling away into the moving parts of a machine, for example, body parts It is unwise for any unauthorized person to remove any guards for any reason.

176) **Q;** What precaution for machine guards for electrical equipment?

A; In addition to safeguarding machinery by mechanical means, the machines which operate by electrical means must be connected correctly, i.e., all machinery which exceeds 42 volts should be connected to an earth-leakage system to prevent electric shock. An earth-leakage system is so designed that any leakage to earth on the tool being used will immediately be detected and the flow of current switched off automatically. In some cases, electrical machinery is double insulated to protect the user from electrical shock. The person installing the machinery must make sure that the machinery has three core wiring, unless of course it is double insulated. In other words, the machinery that is not double insulated must have an earth wire which is usually green/yellow in colour. Usually the blue wire is the neutral wire and the BROWN wire is the live or line wire. The wiring of electrical tools and machinery must be connected correctly.

177) **Q:** What precaution to be taken for portable electrical tools and equipment?

A; Portable electrical tools/machinery must be checked regularly for: loose connections; cracked or broken insulations; earth continuity; switches in bad order; and joins in flexible cords.

178) **Q;** How do you warn employee of faulty electrical equipment or machine?

A: To protect maintenance workers from injury or electric shock from electrical tools and equipment, it may be necessary to place warning notices over machinery to indicate what dangers are latent in the machinery. It may also be necessary to lock the switches to the equipment by padlocks, and only to switch on the equipment where and if necessary. Main switches should be prominently marked.

179) **Q:** What hazards can electrical apparatus cause?

A; Besides electric shock, electricity can also cause external burning, e.g., the arc of a welding machine produces temperatures between 6,000° to 8,000° centigrade. Persons standing nearby such an arc will be severely burnt and such an arc may start a fire by igniting flammable material. When the arc resulting from a breakdown of the insulating material or insulating medium is contained in an enclosure, the heat produced causes the surrounding air or oil to expand rapidly and may also cause an explosion by the expansion of air or oil. Such an explosion can produce extensive damage to property and to persons.

180) **Q**; What causes faulty electrical circuits?

A; Overloading of electrical circuits can produce localised heating of the conductors.

The heat so generated may be sufficient to ignite nearby flammable material and

thus cause a fire, or alternatively, the heating of the conductors may result in a

deterioration of the insulating material and cause a fire.

181) **Q:** What can radiation cause

A; For example, ionising radiation which can cause anaemia, sterility, leukaemia, bone damage, damage to unborn children, genetic damage, tumours, cataracts and shortening of the lifespan; non-ionising radiation such as infra-red and ultraviolet radiation, microwaves, lasers and visible light can produce bums or excessive heating of the skin and tissues just below it. The bums produced vary in their severity according to the extent of the exposure.

182) **Q**: What is the advantage of good Ventilation

A: Proper ventilation is essential to a good environmental health programme. Adequate ventilation and air replacement are necessary for employee health and well-being. One should take advantage of the natural air movement by opening windows or roof monitors. Do not allow ventilation methods to permit noxious fumes or dust to enter the factory- environment from other nearby factories

183) **Q:** What precaution for Power Failures?
A; During power failures, you will not have cooking and lighting facilities. Always have alternative means available such as coal, wood, gas or paraffin. It is always advisable to have candles in the work place or home and battery torches ready for use.

184) **Q:** What to do if refuse is not remove
A; If refuse is not collected, burn or bury refuse. Keep a supply of disinfectant in the house to sprinkle over the refuse before it is buried.

185) **Q:** What you must do in Hurricanes
A; Stay indoors during a hurricane. Take cover under a table or bed. If the roof should be ripped off, these places are the safest.

186) **Q;** What to do in Earthquakes
A; Disconnect all power and gas at once, and evacuate the house or building as quickly as possible. If you are trapped in a house or building, take shelter under a bed or table and protect yourself

against falling objects such as bricks or glass.

187) **Q;** What happened in Floods

A; When floods occur, the Civil Defence will act immediately. Contact the Civil Defence in good time. If you live in a low-lying area, first assist children and elderly persons to higher ground or onto a roof as quickly as possible. Take warm clothing and food to this spot, as well as a torch with which to signal. If time permits, you could also carry some of your possessions to a safe place. Try to divert the water flow with sandbags or other objects at strategic points. Wait for help.

Reference

First Aid

Emergency First Aid for All Ages; First Aid for Babies; First Aid for Teenagers; **First** Aid for Children; Dog First Aid; Work; Emergency First Aid at Work (EFAW) First Aid at Work (FAW) – Regulated Blended Learning; Paediatric First Aid; First Aid for Building & Construction Industry; First Aid for the Beauty Industry;

Food Hygiene

Food hygiene Laws/ regulation 2006 and periodic government guidance note for business example 05/02/2019 and 11/12/2018

Manual handling

Employers must comply with the Manual Handling Operations Regulations 1992, as amended by the Health and Safety (Miscellaneous Amendments) Regulations 2002.

The guidance explains how to avoid, assess and reduce the risk of injury from manual handling.

Health and Safety

Health and Safety at Work etc. Act 1974

The Health and Safety at Work etc. Act 1974 is an Act of the Parliament of the United Kingdom that as of 2011 defines the fundamental structure and authority for the encouragement, regulation and enforcement of workplace health, safety and welfare within the United Kingdom.

Drugs Law

Drugs subject to this Act are known as 'controlled' drugs. The law defines a series of offences including: unlawful supply; intent to supply, import or export and unlawful production. The main difference from the Medicines Act is that the Misuse of Drugs Act also prohibits unlawful possession

INFECTION

Infection control policy is require in every work place

24/07/2015 · Details. The code now reflects the changes required to meet The Health and Social Care Act 2008 (Regulated Activities) Regulations 2014 and the role of infection prevention (including cleanliness) in optimising antimicrobial use and reducing antimicrobial resistance.

Death

Legal death is the recognition under the law of a particular jurisdiction that a person is no longer alive. In most cases, a doctor's declaration of death (variously called) or the identification of a corpse is a legal requirement for such recognition.

INDEX

A – B – C, 246
abdominal, 209, 212, 261
Accident, 29, 247, 248, 249, 250, 281, 299, 335, 359
Acknowledgements, 4
Administration, 16, 17, 18, 75, 76, 122, 135, 141, 144, 145, 146, 147, 148, 150
Aids, 40, 318, 320
Airway, 29, 246
Allergies, 16, 117
Analgesics, 14, 92, 93
Antacids, 14, 92, 94, 100
Ant-depressants, 15, 97
Anti-angina, 14, 92, 94
Anti-arrhythmic, 15, 92, 95
antibiotic, 101

Anti-convulsions, 15, 96, 97
Anti-hypertensive, 15, 99
aromatherapy, 63
Assessing, 33, 183, 270
Association, 45, 363, 365
Auditing, 174, 179
awareness, 111, 242, 243, 344
Bacteria, 21, 25, 102, 184, 186, 187, 211, 212, 214, 224
Benefits, 70
Bereavement, 11, 12
Beta-blockers, 15, 103, 104
Binary, 25, 212, 233
Bleeding, 30, 194, 251, 252
bomb, 39, 307, 312, 313
Breathing, 18, 29, 162, 169, 246
Bronchodilators, 15, 92, 104
Burns, 30, 255
Capsule, 91
chocking, 30
Choking, 260
Clinical, 22, 139, 193, 203
Coding, 46, 368
Communicable, 23, 204
contamination, 156, 192, 198, 211, 214, 218, 220, 222, 224, 225, 231, 235, 238
Contraindications, 16, 116
Controlled, 18, 19, 171, 172, 173
Coroner, 67, 68, 70
COSHH, 40, 41, 42, 182, 192, 194, 201, 285, 316, 335, 336, 338, 339
Danger, 25, 213, 215, 216, 217, 218, 219, 220
Death, 11, 12, 59, 66, 67, 68, 69, 70, 387
Dedication, 4
Defence, 38, 306, 308, 332, 384
Dependence, 16, 119
Diabetes, 15, 31, 105, 262
Diarrhoea, 26, 30, 200, 224, 261
Disclaimer, 3
Diseases, 21, 23, 29, 184, 204, 248, 249, 335, 338
Dishwashers, 27, 229
Disinfecting, 22, 191, 194
Diuretics, 15, 92, 106
dizzy, 98, 99, 258
Donation, 12, 70
Dose, 18, 85, 158, 159, 178
Drugs, 14, 15, 16, 18, 19, 84, 85, 86, 89, 92, 105, 113, 171, 173, 314, 386
Drying, 22, 193, 214, 228
Duties, 25, 33, 206, 269

Dying, 11, 55, 56, 58, 61, 62
Electrocution, 30, 257
Emergency, 18, 158, 242, 318, 370, 385
emetics, 15, 98
enforcement, 230, 386
environment, 36, 37, 39, 44, 82, 83, 147, 182, 188, 193, 243, 245, 251, 264, 282, 284, 290, 292, 296, 303, 308, 310, 321, 323, 324, 332, 335, 345, 348, 349, 358, 359, 365, 383
Environmental, 22, 182, 191, 192, 207, 230
equipment, 27, 35, 36, 37, 41, 44, 46, 47, 82, 136, 138, 166, 167, 168, 169, 170, 182, 183, 188, 191, 192, 193, 196, 198, 202, 206, 210, 226, 227, 238, 239, 251, 269, 270, 281, 282, 285, 289, 290, 291, 292, 293, 294, 295, 296, 297, 298, 302, 317, 321, 322, 324, 325, 330, 331, 333, 334, 338, 346, 348, 358, 359, 361, 366, 367, 369, 370, 372, 373, 374, 375, 379, 380, 381
error, 19, 76, 124, 125, 127, 136, 140, 146, 154, 172, 174, 175, 176, 177, 180, 257, 342
Error, 174, 177
Ethical, 50
Euthanasia, 11, 54
evacuation, 41, 305, 306, 312, 327, 330
Fear, 11, 59, 60
feet, 33, 104, 273, 296, 337, 371, 372
Fire, 2, 41, 245, 326, 327, 329
Fire safety, 2
First Aid, 29, 40, 242, 250, 316, 385
Food, 2, 8, 25, 26, 27, 186, 199, 204, 206, 207, 208, 209, 210, 211, 212, 213, 215, 217, 218, 219, 220, 221, 226, 227, 230, 231, 232, 233, 238, 239, 385, 386
Food hygiene, 2, 199, 207, 386
Fractured, 30, 252
Funeral, 12, 69
GP., 54
Grieving, 12, 72
handling, 33, 46, 162, 164, 189, 193, 199, 200, 203, 204, 206, 208, 214, 222, 223, 224, 226, 245, 251, 269, 270, 272, 371, 386
Hazardous, 14, 21, 83, 184, 197, 285, 339
hazards, 37, 47, 206, 210, 232, 282, 286, 289, 292, 294, 301, 302, 314, 324, 325, 335, 338, 342, 344, 349, 364, 369, 375, 381
headache, 62, 87, 98, 109, 209, 258
Health and Safety, 2, 8, 40, 182, 249, 278, 289, 294, 323, 324, 335, 339, 386
healthcare, 62, 158
Heart, 30, 258
Hepatitis, 204, 320
HIV, 93, 185, 318

house, 35, 75, 281, 282, 383, 384
housekeeping, 35, 36, 152, 192, 281, 282, 283, 338, 348, 363
hypertensive, 99
Immunosuppressant, 15, 93, 106
Inflammatory, 15, 93, 107
Inhaler, 18, 92, 162, 168
Injuries, 21, 29, 184, 248, 249
Intramuscular, 90
Intravenous, 90
Labelling, 17, 142
Law, 7, 21, 25, 183, 206, 207, 386
Laxatives, 15, 93, 107
Legionnaire, 204
Legislation, 14, 21, 38, 81, 182, 306
Lighting, 22, 202, 226, 317
loss, 40, 43, 45, 46, 51, 52, 62, 63, 64, 72, 96, 107, 111, 208, 258, 292, 298, 299, 300, 301, 303, 304, 314, 315, 335, 337, 352, 353, 362, 363, 364, 365, 366
Loss, 11, 51, 52, 63, 64, 353, 360, 361, 362
machines, 46, 192, 292, 367, 374, 376, 378, 380
manual handling, 2, 42, 269, 270, 272, 276, 316, 336, 338, 386
Medication, 13, 14, 16, 17, 18, 19, 75, 76, 78, 83, 84, 85, 88, 89, 90, 91, 92, 110, 112, 120, 123, 124, 126, 128, 129, 130, 134, 137, 138, 141, 143, 145, 146, 150, 151, 152, 155, 157, 162, 166, 167, 174, 177
Migraine, 16, 93, 109
mobility, 52, 63, 100, 110, 253
Mourning, 12, 71
Mouth, 26, 200, 223, 263
Nausea, 12, 64, 96, 209, 259
nose, 26, 91, 141, 168, 198, 200, 212, 223, 246, 252
NSAIDs, 94, 110, 178
Nutritional, 85, 132
Observation, 149
organism, 185
Paediatric, 385
Pets, 23, 26, 186, 204, 211, 225
pharmacist, 78, 83, 112, 115, 116, 125, 126, 127, 128, 143, 151, 156, 159, 162, 164, 165, 173, 176, 177, 180

Physical, 16, 22, 119, 191, 210, 232, 340
Poisoning, 25, 30, 209, 210, 257
Position, 29, 33, 170, 247, 273
PPE, 37, 41, 182, 188, 194, 198, 251, 293, 295, 296, 297, 298, 324, 330, 331
precaution, 36, 46, 47, 284, 285, 288, 372, 374, 379, 380, 383
procedures, 82, 92, 112, 160, 166, 167, 168, 169, 170, 182, 183, 207, 243, 245, 251, 252, 254, 255, 256, 257, 258, 261, 270, 294, 302, 322
Psychological, 119, 361
psychotics, 15, 99, 100
qualifications, 4
Questions, 35, 278
Raw, 211, 227, 234
Recording, 17, 124, 176
Recovery, 29, 72, 247
Reference, 385
reflexology, 63
Registrar, 68, 69
Regulators, 18, 164
requirements, 37, 47, 176, 231, 294, 344, 378
Responsibilities, 14, 21, 82, 183
Resuscitate, 11, 54
Retention, 12, 64
rheumatics, 15, 100
RIDDOR, 41, 182, 248, 249, 335, 338
risk, 33, 36, 42, 46, 83, 98, 105, 110, 112, 113, 114, 115, 119, 130, 134, 154, 164, 175, 178, 183, 198, 208, 209, 213, 216, 234, 238, 243, 262, 269, 270, 272, 276, 277, 282, 289, 298, 305, 315, 318, 330, 331, 334, 335, 338, 339, 340, 341, 355, 366, 367, 369, 386
Shock, 30, 72, 259, 260
Skin, 22, 26, 187, 191, 199, 222, 292
Sluicing, 22, 202
Sources, 14, 78
Specimens, 22, 196
staff, 40, 52, 71, 75, 82, 183, 184, 191, 200, 206, 208, 209, 218, 248, 249, 269, 270, 284, 288, 298, 315, 316, 321, 322, 324, 354
Standards, 38, 300
Staphylococcus, 212, 232, 233
steps, 38, 43, 50, 304, 328, 349, 350, 366
steroids, 15, 104, 172
Stimulants, 16, 108, 111
Storage, 17, 18, 25, 131, 134, 165, 216, 218
Stroke, 30, 258
Subcutaneous, 90
Supervision, 174, 179
Temperature, 25, 169, 206, 216, 217, 234
Terminology, 14, 18, 78, 145
training, 38, 43, 50, 75, 76, 77, 79, 80, 81, 124, 135, 137, 151, 152, 163, 172, 176, 183, 184, 191, 206, 242, 243, 244, 245, 246, 247, 263, 270, 286, 299, 301, 302, 329, 331, 344,

349, 351, 358, 359, 365, 366
Transmission, 21, 187, 188
transplant, 59, 106
unlawful, 386
User, 52, 54, 55, 56, 58, 60, 61, 62, 63, 64, 65, 188, 189, 193, 198, 199, 202, 248
ventilation, 22, 192, 202, 218, 226, 284, 288, 317, 325, 382
Victim, 44, 360
Viruses, 21, 184, 185
Vitamins, 16, 93, 112
Waste, 22, 23, 27, 183, 188, 203, 204, 229, 238
Water, 12, 64, 186, 261, 326, 327
Zone, 25, 213, 215, 216, 217, 218, 219, 220

Printed in Great Britain
by Amazon

25093926R00225